"It's impossible," said pride.
"It's risky," said experience.
"It's pointless," said reason.
"Give it a try," whispered the heart.
~ Unknown

PRAISE FOR JULIEANNE O'CONNOR'S
SPELLING IT OUT FOR YOUR MAN

"Julieanne O'Connor uses heart, humor and life experience to help us navigate the, often times, choppy waters of relationships. Like having a conversation with your best friend, she answers all of the questions you've ever asked (or were too embarrassed to ask) about being satisfied and happy in love. Woman or man, young or old, in love or ready to be, you will find something to relate to in *Spelling It Out for Your Man*." – Kym Lamison, Former owner of *Central Coast News Group*

"*Spelling It Out for Your Man* is the GPS for a Man lost in a sea of relationships. Julieanne is my Oracle for women... I experienced her genius first hand when she literally took my cell phone and started texting things I'd never say to this girl I was seeing. I couldn't believe the results that were obviously positive. I was instantly empowered and in awe." –Kevin Laird, Analyst and Father

"THIS BOOK IS A MUST for any Woman who wants to know what her man is thinking or feeling, how to react in any given situation, how to stay true to herself always, and how to be a whole person with or without him. Because at the end of the day, if you're not happy with yourself, how can you be happy with someone else? Let this book be your 'Dating/Relationship Bible.' Read it a few times. Refer back to it when needed. Just like the author Julieanne, this book is a treasure." –Tiffany Phillips, Comedian, Writer and Star of *I Never Met a Jerk I Didn't Like*

"*Spelling It Out for Your Man* helped me to recognize and reflect upon some of the negative cycles and behaviors that I have fallen into in my relationship, and the book offered solutions and philosophies that changed my pattern of thinking and has helped me to improve my romance." –Robbie Gilmartin, Teacher, Coach and Author of *Enhancing Self-Esteem Through Guided Imagery*

"Julieanne has a knack for digging out the raw truth and she has no problem making you cry as long as you face your truth. She has turned both men and women around in their relationships. *Spelling It Out for Your Man* will keep you running back for her brilliant insights." –Mark O'Connor, Marine, Husband and Father

"In life what matters most are relationships. With your God, with your spouse, with your loved ones, friends, co-workers and most importantly, yourself. I have been both blessed and blissed to have been touched by Ms. O'Connor's infectious enthusiasm for life. Regardless of who she meets, they immediately fall in love with her! Why is that? She has mastered the art of creating immediate trusting mutually beneficial relationships. In her book, *Spelling It Out for Your Man*, she holds back no punches. She tells us straight, as men, how to best treat and understand our ladies. She tells our ladies, how to best guide us men, not to be such jerks at times! This is a MUST READ for anyone who wants more joy, more abundance and more energy in their relationships. –Jeffrey A. Forrest, Author, Speaker and Safe Money for Life Coach

"Oh boy did *Spelling It Out for Your Man* ever teach me about giving a man SPACE and the impact it can have on attraction. It is packed full of truth. As a woman, I think I might actually hate the word "space." LOL. In all seriousness, the book is right on the point. In fact so much so I am hiding it from the man I want back. He will definitely get ideas from it that I'm not ready to share. –Bonnie Pitkin, Artist

SPELLING IT OUT FOR YOUR MAN

Insider Secrets to Sex, Love and Attraction for Men and Women

By Julieanne O'Connor

Martin Sisters Publishing

Published by

Martin Sisters Publishing, LLC

www. martinsisterspublishing. com

Copyright © 2013 Julieanne O'Connor

ISBN: 978-1-62553-056-1

Nonfiction
Mainstream/Inspirational
Printed in the United States of America
Martin Sisters Publishing, LLC

DEDICATION

This book is dedicated to my incredible husband Mark and my gifted, spirited, and angelic daughter Lotus for allowing me to breathe into the space of living and loving by choice. They are my daily reason for everything I do.

ACKNOWLEDGMENTS

For all my girlfriends. For Tiffany Phillips who has *"Never Met a Jerk She Didn't Like."* For Melissa who has left a trail of broken hearts along her path. For Tia who is smart. For those of you who have shown us all what <u>not</u> to do with a man. For Heather T. for hysterical memories. For Tess who waited and then pounced on the right guy and also for becoming one of my dearest friends. For JR, for being the right guy. For Kati and Rex. For Pam and Jeff Forrest for so many reasons I lost count. For Jennifer and Jason. For Kara. For Summer. For Kevin Laird for testing my theories. For Garry Banks for divulging his dating stories. For Scott O'Connor for sharing his study of the game. For Lacie for seeing that love is limitless. For Matt. For Wally and Joann. For Wallace and Caitlin. For Dick and Kathy. For Gol and Pierre. For John. For Claire, Audra and Anne. For Kandice. For Bill Chuck. For Paul and Mandy. For Reese and Tammy who I miss with my whole heart. For Steven Van Heusen for his never-ending goodness. For Mary. For Jay. For Hot Coffee. For Tamara. For Erika. For Keith Smith. For Edna. For Mark and Chris H. For Mike and Kristen for giving so much love to the children. For Mike and Heather. For Jennifer and Michael. For Scott and Ann. For Patrick and Stacey. For Ali, Melanie and Kelly. For Debbie T, Jennifer B. and Melissa M. For Pete and Denise. For Tim and Heidi. For Kevin West. For Michael and Dawn. For Jessica, Angel and Alex. For Eileen, Shirley and Anthony. For Danielle and Allen. For Clarissa. For Tommy. For Sam and Jeanette. For Mikey H. For Dave R, Dave B, and Dave D. For Tom Ratiner. For Paul M. For Jeremy Koff. For Rodney De Caussin. For my dear friend David Hughes, wherever you are. For Kidney Beans. For Chad and Katie. For Leatta. For Kym. For Snowmen. For Gia. For Shana. For Russel, Angi and the kids. For

Stokely. For Anthony Meindl. For Christopher and Tyler. For Gregory. For Zach. For Jennifer P. For Zeke. For Mark and Tracy Jarvis. For Jeff Gross. For Mr. Pibbles. For Richard E. For Jeff Goldblum. For Russell T and his family. For Thomas. For Smo. For Bioseh and Hannah. For Andre. For Joe C. For Allen R and his family. For Steve and Julie L. For Brian W. For Tex Barrett. For Joe. For Terrell. For Fanci. For Fatima wherever you are. For Debra. For Renee and Ben. For Zen. For Rebo. For Broderick J. For Bob M. For Bo. For Brent and Cammie. For Kipp. For Nate and Haley. For Gary and Melissa. For Dolores and Werner for sharing the joy that comes from making each other number one. For Tyson and Melissa. For Kevin and Danielle. For Jeff and Andrea. For Craig and Kim. For Mark and Sandra. For Diane and Craig. For Linda, Dan, Daniel and Randi. For George and Renie. For Aunt Nancy. For Nancy and Barbara. For Bob and Judy. For Tyler and Chelsea. For Aymee and Mark Frassica. For everyone from LBD. For Chris and Julie Cucchiara. For Candy. For Ken K. For Fig Leaves. For Daniel & his family. For everyone at The Legacy Partners. For everyone at HH. For Enlightened Warriors. For everyone at Faller & Joiner, LLP. For everyone at Toastmasters Club 83. For Syd. For Matt, Sandy and the kids. For Wade. For Dirk. For Dona Mitchell. For Michelle R. For Angel P and family. For Angeilique Craven. For Diana Gunbjornsen. For Fred Jung. For Aaron Ball. For Stefan. For Angeleaque & Avery Raulston. For Kolt, Lucky, Morgan, Kalei, Thachary and Sunny. For Helga. For Uncle Bruce. For Bruce (Boofie) and Kathy. For Earl. For Ward. For Luis and Regina. For Martin. For Lou Dog wherever you are. For Donna Ducharme. For Linda. For Mark Blake Management – Mark, you rock! For Annie Schwartz, Tim O'Shea and Marc Chancer at Origin Talent – THANK YOU!

For ALL of my family and friends, and for all of Mark's. For all the guys who taught me well. For all my one-night stands. For those who married smart and those who settled short. For all who married for money. And for those who have been blessed with their soul mates.

For anyone and everyone experiencing intolerance related to your choice in love. May things change before your very eyes, leaving you free to express your love openly, free from judgment.

In memory of my Dad, Uncle Jim, Aunt Vicki, Vikki, Maxine, Betty, James, Justin, Dr. Frank Ryan, Nigel Hawthorne, Gina Mastrogiacomo, my Grandparents, Charlie, and those friends who transitioned by choice. Also in memory of Mohammed, Magic, Meta, O'Grrr, Hannibal, Emily, Winston, Sadie, and Cici.

For my dear sister Robbie, who risked it all for love. For Marvin and his children. For my gorgeous baby sister Amber, who loves fully and who will release her own book one day. For Dave and David. For all the people who shared with me their secret to a happy marriage. For my mom, for everything that she is, everything that she continues to be, and for advising me to drop everything to follow my heart. For my kind-hearted father Gary who always laughs and plays. For my dad, Robert who showed me that love lives on forever. For the broken-hearted and for those in-love.

For my beautiful, expressive, kind loving, courageous daughter Lotus who will approach this unchartered territory with bright eyes and an angel's heart. There will be a time when love is beautiful and passionate and nothing else will exist but you and the person you love, and a time when love hurts so badly that you will wish you wouldn't wake up. I say this. Always, always, always approach love with the heart of the angel you were born with. Never become bitter and always know that pain goes away. Marry for love. But also choose to marry a man or woman who you love that treats you with the ultimate respect for your expression of who you are at your very core. Always see the good, appreciate every moment and remember that love lives on forever.

For my husband Mark who always stands by me through my most unbridled and outrageous moments and who always stands-up for my expression of self. For loving me and treating me like a Goddess even when PMS and a full moon both fall on the same day. For being a joy to spend every day with, for always choosing me over "the guys" and "other women," and for the best conversation and inspiration a girl could hope for. Thank you for being a man who truly never falls short of the masculine being I so crave in my life and for making me feel beautiful, sexy and always special. Thank you for dreaming big with me.

> For those who hurt and those who cared
> For those who took and those who shared
> For those who are good and those who are bad
> For those who laugh and those who are sad
> For those who are bitter and those who are new
> For those who are smiling and those who are blue
> For those who are lucky and those who are not
> For those who are seekers and those who are sought
> For all of the boyfriends who trained me
> For those who let me be
> For my incredible husband, the man of my dreams
> Who showed me in life it's not all what it seems
> Always be open to the beauty you see
> And live your life with the best of chi
> But above all else share your heart
> With the one who you love, do not be apart.
> *Life is Love!*

Whether you love men or women and whether you're a man or a woman, I honor those who love and those who risk it all for love. I honor those who choose wisely a loving partner who accepts the true you without regard for race, religion, sexual orientation or other discriminatory bias. We will all experience the judgment of others when we fall in love. Love with your whole being anyway. Men and women can both have masculine and feminine qualities. If you are a man who finds yourself more on the feminine side of things or you are a woman who finds yourself more on the masculine side of things, please read this book with the idea in mind that I share the extremes of masculinity vs. femininity in relationships as referenced by men vs. women but you can place yourself anywhere on the scale of either gender that makes sense for you. We are all individuals so generalizations may not always apply.

To love without ownership, to love with total trust and faith in that very love, to love with the same faith you have that your heart will keep beating moments from now, that is the ultimate love.

"I dreamed a dream with no boundaries and it was of a life I desired with a mate who completed me. It was received. But then I began to manipulate my own manifestation to take me back to my formerly believed world, my man-made comfort zone. I then imposed my restricted beliefs on my significant other who I soon forgot was his own person, and so I pushed him away.

Then I opened my eyes and noticed that life needs no limitations and suddenly I again re-created my universe, only with more beauty and more freedom, as I realized I could. I became a builder, an artist, a lover, happy. And my new love was handed his wings."

Thank you to the Napoleon Hill Foundation (naphill.org) for your consent to use select quotes within this book. Thank you

Timber Hawkeye (buddhistbootcamp.com) for your guidance. Thank you Belinda Osborne for your commitment to helping promote this book.

Thank you Seth Rogen for being so cool and for the ultimate quote. Thank you Steve Martin for your humor. Thank you J.Z. Colby for your great writing and your unbelievable generosity. Thank you Jarod Kintz. Thank you Paul Sloane. Thank you Mariel Hemingway.

Thank you to my editor, Kathleen Papajohn.

Thank you Melissa Newman and Martin Sisters Publishing, Inc. (martinsisterspublishing.com) for believing in this book.

CONTENTS

PART FIVE
Common Mistakes

PART SIX
Insights On and For Men

PART SEVEN
I Got Needs, and They're Multiplying

PART EIGHT
When to Throw in the Towel

PART NINE
Hurt, Open, Heal, Open

PART TEN
Attitude, Gratitude, Makes Your Life

PART ELEVEN
Spelling It Out, A Life Fulfilled

INTRODUCTION

"Art has one purpose, that is to leave you changed.
Love has one purpose, that is to create art."
~ Julieanne-ism

If you speak three languages you're trilingual. If you speak two languages you're bilingual. If you speak the language of the opposite sex, you can communicate.

Once upon a time, a beautiful princess was born. She grew up out of the muck of life and blossomed into a gorgeous young lady. She learned to cook and clean, sing and dance, smile and express herself, nurture and care for others, but most of all she dreamed about her perfect Prince Charming, always knowing in her heart that he too was somewhere dreaming of her. She knew one day she would have the perfect fairy tale wedding and live happily ever after.

Nearby in a regular ol' village of ordinary people, there lived a strong and handsome man. He worked hard while frequently saving the day by fixing life's daily tragedies. All the women loved him, and would say anything that they thought he wanted to hear, just to have the chance that maybe one day he might whisper something sweet in return.

One day the handsome young man ran abruptly into the gorgeous princess and both were knocked off their feet by an inexplicable force unimaginable by most mortal beings. He whisked her up with his strong arms and spun her around setting her gently onto his white horse-drawn carriage as it magically appeared before them, and they rode off into the sunset.

Only a few months went by before they were seen again at which time they rode back into the small village accompanied by a crowd of people singing and dancing as they celebrated their magical day and were married.

The very next day the prince awoke to his gorgeous princess

and noticed she was even more beautiful than he had realized, seeing her now for the first time ever, with no makeup. He began basking silently in this blessing that had been bestowed upon him.

The beautiful princess, worrying that she might not look as good as she should without her makeup, noticed that her man went suddenly quiet at her sight. She quickly hid her face and ran off to beautify herself.

Not knowing why she ran away, the young man decided he would build a castle to surprise his new princess proving his undying love. In so doing he began spending hours away from her, giving everything he had to accomplish this massive feat.

Each day the princess began to grow more uptight as her man would return home late and exhausted. She would immediately run to him at the door and begin sharing every small detail of her day.

Exhausted from a hard day's work and knowing his need to replenish his energy the man would abruptly forget his wife was talking, and then suddenly notice as she stomped away oddly emotional. Knowing that as a man he would want to be left alone during an unexplainable moment of unhappiness, he would give her plenty of space to work through whatever it was that she must have going on.

Meanwhile the princess sobbed as she noticed that her man failed to run after her, as she would have done if the circumstances had been reversed. She quickly drew the conclusion that he must not love her anymore.

Soon the man was greeted by an incessantly unhappy woman who pointed out his daily flaws and he realized his princess was increasingly displeased by his every action. So he began to work harder still with even longer days away in an attempt to finish the castle once and for all. At last he spent one final day working around the clock, only this time not returning home through the night in order to wrap up every fine detail with precision. The final touches of candles, chocolates, roses, fine wine and music were added and at last it was ready to present to his lady.

It was complete and he rode home quickly to share this magnificent gift with his love of his life. Only upon his arrival to their humble prior home, he was not greeted by his wife at all. As he called out for her, he heard only the echo of emptiness. What had happened he wondered scratching his head? Where had she gone? And he was lost.

Now this is no ordinary story as it turns out. This is a common tale which now occurs in the majority of marriages today. Only this particular story just happens to be one of those stories where you, the reader gets to choose the ending.

Ladies, do you have the fairy tale relationship or are you wondering if it's true, what all men want? Are you curious why your man continuously fails to pick up on seemingly obvious hints? Are you a man trying to please your un-please-able woman? Or a man who is wondering what happened to that sexy hot babe you originally started dating? Are you a man or a woman who is in love with someone with whom you can't or shouldn't be with? Do you ever find yourself saying things like… "Really?!" "Seriously?!" "Are you kidding me?!" or more often than not, "WTF?!" as you attempt to get on the same page with your significant other? Do you ever find yourself advising others about their obviously poor relationship choices? If you are a man or a woman and you would like to experience a few profound "ah-ha's" about relationships, or even simply confirm what you already know to be true, you have come to the right place. Men and women, boys and girls – here's the map to your fairy tale!

Most issues in relationships begin with the most fundamental missed steps that men consistently repeat over and over. Yes, that's right! It's the man's fault. It's true. However, it's the women who drive the men to act the way they do or moreover the women who have the chance to quickly simplify everything. One woman can have a profound effect on a guy by following a few simple, though sometimes seemingly unnatural, easy steps. For a woman it can be as simple as "spelling it out

for your man!" Men want their women happy. If they don't –
run! But most guys are simply missing the mark (the actual
definition of sinning)!

If you are a man, pull out a highlighter. If you are a woman,
take notes and implement these simple practices, with guts. In
order to spell it out for your man, it requires some no-
nonsense, no bullshit moves that can change your life forever.

1

What's Love Got to Do with It? Love Basics

CAKE AND EAT IT TOO

"You can't have your cake and eat it too."
~ English Proverb

"Sex without love is as hollow and ridiculous as love without sex."
~ Hunter S. Thompson

Life is surreal. When you step back and really take a look at it, the irony is absolute. Yes, it's true, men want to have their cake and eat it too. Who doesn't?

When men think of intimacy, they think of the physical act of closeness, or more bluntly, they think of banging some hot babe. When women think of intimacy, they think of connecting emotionally. Both men and women want to experience

23

emotional and sexual connectedness but men come to the emotional side after sexual arousal whereas women desire sexual intimacy only after first connecting emotionally. That does not however, mean a woman should give up her body to gain a man's affection, as there is significant risk in losing his interest by doing so too quickly. In fact, for ladies, the longer you can hold out, the more a guy will generally respect you and in fact, maybe indefinitely. My feeling on the subject of sex with a man is - don't give it up unless you're willing to give him up. Not in the beginning. Sex is power!

You might already be asking yourself if it's TRUE what they say about "what all men want?" The answer is yes! Men are not complicated and once you understand this, there is tremendous freedom in owning this knowledge. In fact, by accepting this sometimes disturbing information you will be empowered to play an effective game of intimacy to your advantage without ever having to announce your brilliant insight into the subject. Most men know deep down what they really want but are forced to compromise in today's society, giving ladies all the advantage. This goes unrealized by most ladies. Men generally don't talk about what they secretly fantasize about and certainly rarely speak of it to women. The exceptions are in the case of great comedians or swingers and occasionally a guy who trusts a girl enough to open up and really talk dirty, nearly always in secrecy.

Here's the irony. A guy wants to be "the good guy" or "the great catch!" He wants to marry his perfect queen and wants to be a powerful man worthy of devoted love and attention by one exceptional lady, and preferably one who is a virgin who will ravish him like the most seasoned stripper. Simultaneously, and herein lies the chaos surrounding men, a typical man would also like the option to have a hot torrid affair with any beautiful girl that crosses his path. It's quite a lot of turmoil to live with if you really think about it. Imagine how pulled you might feel. Wanting to be true to your very nature which is at least partly in conflict with that which is expected of you by your society and the very female beasts you are most driven by.

At the end of the day, men can only have it one way or the other and yet they truly wish they could have both. A man has to eventually compromise or he is considered a "cheater" or a "womanizer." To avoid the labels the majority of men settle down or sometimes become quite sneaky, which is probably fairly easy to get away with given men rarely have a habit of over-talking. That or they become dissatisfied and therefore often depressed. Unless of course a woman can keep him satisfied or he channels his sexual drive into something more dangerous.

One poll I read said that 60% of married men had cheated or had an affair, while 40% of married women had supposedly had an affair. I assure you that the reasons for men and women's affairs are quite different. When a lady has an affair on her partner, it's because she has connected with someone who has made her feel sexy, beautiful, wanted or heard. For a guy, more than likely, he just simply wanted to get laid. Problem for men in the cheating department is that women come with drama. Remember, a lady has sex after she's connected emotionally which means, after the sex, she's probably not going away that easily. Therein lies the problem with cheating for a man with a wife.

Unlike men who really want to score their dream wife while simultaneously wishing they could have unlimited hot sex with others, women are *driven* to find their soul mates, marry them and live happily ever after. They strive to get exactly what they want with zero compromise and fight every inch of the way for what they are after. Unfortunately, often this ends in a sobbing defeat for the ladies until they wise up to the ways of men. If we could all have this spelled out to us early in life, we'd probably have a lot more successful relationships as we'd take everything less personally.

Ladies, you have a ton of power if you just understand the fundamental differences between men and women and unaffectedly play by the rules. After all, women are also simple.

I know the guys are saying to themselves, "Whoa, what do you mean women are simple? What a lie!" But it's true. The good thing is ladies do not have to live with any turmoil or conflict about this. We know exactly what we want! There's no dichotomy of nature bestowed upon us because of our current society. Nope, we know exactly what we want and society currently dictates that women are in the right! Women deserve a good guy who settles down, marries them, provides for them and protects them, makes them feel special and LISTENS to them. Screech halt. Now the ladies are saying "WHOA, I don't have all that in my marriage." Or the ladies are still young and hopeful. Note: Society may not always dictate that the rules remain as they currently are where a man is supposed to settle down with one woman. It certainly wasn't that way in the past, but right now in today's society a lady has an advantage if she is just willing to please her man.

The issues for women typically stem from a lack of understanding about the nature of men and from a lack of willpower. The bigger issue usually being willpower. Once you even slightly get a handle on this, you will unleash new powers you never thought you had. Women's instincts are keen and often we know what we should do. Unfortunately, we just can't seem to resist the urge to do things contrary to what's best for us. Typically we commit these breaches to our own better judgment in an attempt to get some quick satisfaction in the area of reassurance, or to boost our own egos. However, these acts we commit in an attempt to get reassurance are the very things that take our power away. You've heard the sayings about those things worth getting are worth waiting for. This is no different. Usually the hardest path will bring the greatest reward.

Ladies should always resist the urge to drop hints to get reassurance from men. The only effective way to get a man's attention or reassurance is to literally spell it out for him. Men do not get hints. They are devoid of the "hint" gene. For the record once and for all, they really don't get it. Women want so badly to believe that men pick up on subtle clues given to them and often women use this against them when communication doesn't elicit a desired response. Let's face it, it's not their fault. They are men. Again, men were born with<u>out</u> the "hint" gene intact. It really was cut along with the umbilical cord at birth. Catching on to hints for a man is much like a woman comprehending a man who has just started a sentence out of left field with ZERO context, expecting her to JUMP IN and understand what he's referencing without further explanation.

That brings me back to the nature of men. We ladies have to take it easy on men because though they know what they want deep down, they live in a constant state of conflict between being who they really are, and still trying to fit in with what is expected of them by both women and society. It must be frustrating at times if you really think about it. The only reason that men become complicated in our minds is because we neglect some basic principles when dealing with them. Men will tell you this as well. It's up to us women to take responsibility for our own actions in a relationship. Then maybe the men will take more responsibility as well. Men, if you want to help out, feel free to jump in and give us ladies some added reassurance before we come begging for it. We prefer not to have to spell this need out.

Women in committed relationships truly do have the upper hand if only they realize it. They can fully call the shots if they know how to keep their man happy. One reason that a man who is in a committed relationship may actually think that he's <u>in control</u> in a relationship is because he has tired of trying to deal with a women's inability to satisfy his most basic needs and so he throws his hands up and begins calling the shots.

If a man is calling all the shots in a relationship it's usually mixed with a state of guilt or dissatisfaction that prevents him from finding pleasure in his own nature. Men do appreciate women who can hold their own. A guy calling the shots simply means a guy who is telling a girl what to do, cheating, disappearing for his vices more than spending time with his woman, etc. Often the guilty state that follows these actions will lead a man to non-responsiveness or exaggerated attempts to over compensate for his guilt about his actions. We all know how annoying that can be and certainly a man will simultaneously be less attracted to his woman. So if you're currently a woman who is with a guy who is running the show, you are not as hot as you potentially could be right now!

A quick point of clarification regarding the subject of "calling the shots:" When I talk about a woman calling the shots or having the upper hand in a relationship, I do mean from an existential point of view. Think in terms of your female sexuality and the power it has over a man. I do NOT mean calling the shots by telling a man how to do everything. Men need to manufacture their own testosterone by being allowed to save the day, fix things, build things and live without women telling them every step of the way how to do everything. Even if this means you can plainly see a man is about to mess up, at least sometimes they need to be allowed to do so without a woman's constant instruction. "Calling the shots" should be give and take in any relationship. When a man is calling ALL the shots, his woman will definitely be less attractive to him. A woman needs to possess some sexual prowess over a man. Certainly a little of this in the reverse scenario is nice as well. While balancing this interaction we ladies need to keep in mind the difference between being annoyingly bossy and being mysteriously in control of our own being, body and sexuality. That is the fine line I'm referring to when I reference "calling the shots." It is not a matter of telling someone what to do, though this may at times come into play in the appropriate context. It is about owning your own essence without being completely dependent upon the man you long for.

Love basics start with the willingness to consider our partner's point of view while maintaining our own self-worth. This often leads to a willingness to learn how to meet each other's needs prior to our own. If at this point you are wondering what loves got to do with it, just hang tough and soon enough you will see. It is undeniable that we all make mistakes in relationships from time to time. The key is in practicing what we already know deep down we are capable of. For some this can be more uncomfortable than for others, as many have made a habit out of mistakes. When the mistakes have been perpetuated in a relationship for a long period of time, it may take longer for a partner or love interest to notice the positive changes. But rest assured, consistency in channeling self-worth and sexuality while considering others' perspectives will get a person noticed. For some this could be scary while for others it will be a ridiculous ton of fun.

OBVIOUS CHOICES

> *"The great discoveries are usually obvious."*
> ~ *Phil Crosby*

> *"A day without sunshine is like, you know, night."*
> ~ *Steve Martin*

Be willing to walk away before you arrive! That's confidence. If you are currently in the single and selecting stage, please heed the following warnings. Here are some fundamental obvious choices and mistakes that both men and women frequently make in selecting a mate. If you are involved in a committed relationship where you have already made some of the choices I'm about to mention, stand by for upcoming tips on how to make adjustments within the parameters of an already established relationship. First, let's talk about obvious choices.

Ladies:

1. If a guy says he does <u>NOT</u> want a relationship... LISTEN to him! Do not get intimately involved if you yourself are in fact personally looking for a committed

relationship. You can't believe how many women break this fundamental and yet obvious rule.

2. If a guy clearly has a wife and kids and has stated he does not want more children, but you in fact would like to have a baby, the "wife" part aside, WALK AWAY!

3. If a guy is married or living with a girlfriend of 9 years, give or take, and you are hoping he will leave his girl, it is not likely! If you absolutely must get involved, have your fun but then walk away. Better yet, just walk away. If he does by some rare act of fate become single, then you will have your shot to see if he's the one at that time. This may come as a blow to some women, but there's a good chance with a guy who is cheating that there have been other girlfriends before you and there could be more after you. This can actually apply to both sexes.

4. If a guy loves his sports, drinks, smokes, video games, or happens to have some other annoying habit that you really can't stand, know that ALL MEN have some of these habits. Choose wisely a guy with habits which you can tolerate without it driving you to become a nag.

5. If you live in Southern California and your man lives in Spain and you would really like a committed relationship for life, consider a move or move on.

Men:

1. Forget everything you've heard about what women want. A woman wants a guy who is so madly confident he is willing to walk away before he arrives. A woman doesn't want a guy who is too overly willing to accommodate her in the beginning. A woman is turned-on by the chase but will be the first to protest that she doesn't want to play games. So keep in mind that the game of the "chase" has to be played whether you think it does or not.

2. If a girl looks you in the eyes during sex and says she is climaxing, she may be lying. Just go with it.
3. If a girl doesn't call you back or gives you excuses why she can't see you, she may not actually want to see you. Walk away and give her space or ask her if you did something wrong.
4. Even if you're in the friend zone, if you stop calling a girl, she will eventually miss you and call. When she calls, be sure to own your masculinity and do not reply too anxiously. Hold back, play it cool and have your own thing going on.
5. Even the shortest, fattest, baldest and oldest guy can be a perfect fit for a hot smart girl if he is extremely secure with himself, fun and funny, and exudes confidence without arrogance. On the flip side a guy can be totally hot and attractive, then open his mouth and completely blow it. Simply harness your assets and know your own value. Exude confidence without arrogance and trust that no one is out of your league if you play your cards right.
6. What a girl says is not necessarily what she means. Don't assume you know what she is talking about without verifying. Be wise and seek clarification before drawing conclusions.

Though this list of "obvious" rules could be converted into a book of its own, I will keep it short. Simple advice, if it is obviously a wrong choice, walk away before you fall. If you have already fallen, do not panic, this book will help you through the process to change your circumstances for the better. Just because you want to believe something, doesn't mean it's true. Be patient and kind with yourself as with every rule, there are always exceptions.

THE RECURRING THEME

*"I believe that sex is one of the most beautiful, natural,
wholesome things that money can buy."*
~Steve Martin

"If he would just touch me in the right places at the right time…"
~Anonymous Woman

"If she would just touch me at all…"
~Anonymous Man

"Sex? What's that?"
~Anonymous Married Man

Without touch, did you know that the brain develops abnormally and infants that have received food and shelter but no touch have actually died without this basic need met? All humans need to be touched.

Is making love a job? Is anyone tired of it? Do you wish your partner wanted it more? Do you just want to be cuddled? Do you wish your woman would ravish you? Has your man stopped kissing you the way you want him to kiss you?

I had the most enlightening talk with a married man who married a smoking hot woman. They are both lifeguards and enjoy their work. He's been married a while now and loves his wife and family. There is no question in anyone's mind that he found his "trophy" wife. She's the girl a guy wants on his shoulder. All the men think she's hot. Everyone thinks she must be especially hot in the bedroom as she walks around with an intensity that oozes that of a powerful hot woman. You assume she would naturally enchant her partner behind closed doors. Other women are positively scared of this lady. I myself included. She has the vibe that she'd rip your heart out if you looked at her man wrong. It turns out she actually would rip someone's heart out according to her husband; however, she is nothing that you'd expect in the bedroom.

According to her man, this woman treats sex like a less than satisfying job. To her it is what she has to do to please her man but there is no ownership of her personal sexuality backing it. She hates the idea of porn because she thinks it's slutty. Yet her man likes porn for one main reason. He said it has nothing to do with how hot the women are. It is simply because they ACT like *"they WANT IT."* He cannot understand why his girl won't beg for sex or at least play the part of a girl who can't live without his body. He wants his girl to be confident with her body and to ACT like she loves everything about sex with him. Instead, she simply gives it up without the tease, without the game and without playing with him or being sensual. Then she says to him repetitively that she doesn't feel like he loves her enough. She just wants to cuddle and be held without any sexual advances. This terribly unsatisfied guy shared all of these details with me but admitted he had never tried spelling it out for his wife. Evidently when either tries to express their needs to the other, it is done in an offensive or defensive state and lacks clarity. Never in a neutral tone with the intent to share in the responsibility of meeting each other's needs.

If you are reading this and wondering why this guy can't give this girl more love or if you're wondering why this girl can't own her own hot body and therefore give her man more hot sex, let me elaborate. Generally speaking, women are emotional. Men are more visual and sexual. There are of course variations with both sexes where some men are more emotional and some women are more sexual. But generally, feeling love leads women to own their sexuality and getting hot sex leads men to give more love. Sounds simple but when you're wired one way, it can seem like work to do the opposite to get your needed end result. Both love and sex beget each other. If you are hoping to get one without giving the other you will neglect nature's need for balance in these areas of intimacy. Much of this is like acting and becoming a professional at the part you need to play. In other words men need to play the part of the nurturing loving gentle cuddly but confident protector guy and women need to play the part of the sensual sexual desiring woman who can't live without her man's penis. The common problem is that as human beings we have a tendency to focus on what we ourselves need, thinking that we'll give a person what they need right after we get what we want. This leads to a stale mate.

My day wrapped up at a conference where I met several more young men who had been married anywhere from 5-10 years and who had the same complaints. Their wives didn't touch them. They were bored. They desired sex with other women. Yet they could not fathom their wives leaving them to be with other men. You may be asking yourself how this topic comes up at a conference. Let me just say this. It is extremely easy to disarm men about this subject when you take an interest in sex and express your non-judgment about the obvious common thread.

There are a few men reading this who don't have this problem of wishing they got more hot sex. I assure you those are the guys who are newly married, just about to get married or simply dating. That or they have already mastered communication with their partner. This subject is nearly full proof. Not kidding if I survey 1000 men, I'll hear small variations of the exact same theme. For women the variations are slightly different. With women sometimes the issue is the need for more love and snuggling while other times the issue is in fact the quality of sex. Most men do not realize how much most women love sex under the right conditions.

There are some fundamental things that make sex more exciting for women that many men are not aware of. For example, women don't need to connect emotionally with their men when trying to have an orgasm (we do this for the men). One exception to this is when we are at very first in a newly blissful madly passionate relationship where sometimes we can in fact get off while staring a man in the face. If it were up to us with men that we've been with for a long time, we'd be blind folded when we had sex so we could live out our never ending faux pas sexual fantasies. These are the fantasies that we'd usually never admit to anyone. These are the fantasies that are instantly destroyed when we have to look a man in the eyes. This does not necessarily apply in the case of sex with strangers. Truthfully, if it were up to us, we'd be ravished by the hot massage therapist in an exotic place where no one would ever know that he or she took advantage of us, for example.

Women don't need to know that men want sex, we already know it. Assuming we are in the mood, we just need to know that someone's confident enough to take us and pleasure us. (Caution, a guy must ensure that a woman consents when this is happening). We love to be taken advantage of (by our choice, so we are clear) so that we can surrender to a no-guilt hot sexual experience where we are forced to be pleasured. Don't freak out, I'm not saying we desire to be raped. This has to be a safe environment to live out our fantasies. We do not get off if we are feeling pressure to do so, nor if we are connecting in an emotionally intense connection that makes us self-aware, nor if we are feeling at all self-conscious in general. If any of this is happening and we still appear to be getting off, I assure you we are likely faking it.

About pleasuring a woman, and yes, this is where I spell it out for the men. You may have witnessed a woman getting herself off at some point. Do not attempt to recreate what you've seen. What gets a woman off when pleasuring herself is not easily done by someone else. What a woman needs from a man or partner is light touch, and avoidance of immediate touch to the most intimate spots. She needs a man to tease her. The more foreplay the better. A massage for example can arouse a woman much more quickly than penetration. Women like to be lightly touched everywhere around their most cherished spots. Sometimes women prefer to be touched by something other than the man's hand or body. This can be true with oral as well. A man should kiss and touch gently everywhere but the most intense places initially. Get us worked

35

up so we do beg you for it. If you are a man reading this, now you know. The more you tease us prior to penetration, the more likely you will be to get us off, or get us to beg you for it. We love to be teased by touch. This also gives us enough time to get out of our head (meaning out of our regular thinking) and begin to imagine those hot scenarios that we'll likely never admit turn us on.

A final note on this: Sometimes, women are not in the mood. However, even though we are not in the mood to have an orgasm, we still often want to please our man. We enjoy the sex but we are not likely going to get off. In these cases, it's OK for the man to just handle his business and not feel guilty about whether or not he pleased his woman. We may in fact rather you just hurry it up. I realize it's confusing but again, know that we still enjoy the sex. We just aren't in it to have an orgasm at the time. Enjoy and be done! Ladies, relieve your man of his manly duties when this is the case by spelling it out for him to let him know that it's OK for him to enjoy himself. Describe your expectations. Do not expect him to guess.

Men want women to want them so much that they beg for it. Women want men to adore, love, sometimes cuddle, and definitely tease them before sex. If each were willing to give the other what they wanted, both would more likely find that they too would receive what they needed. It is up to each of us to take responsibility for initiating what our partner needs to then get what we most desire. Keep in mind; none of us are mind readers. The most sure-way to get what you need, is to spell it out for each other. Describe to your partner what turns you on. What makes you willing to give your partner what they need? Give your partner details so they understand how you are programmed. When dealing with the opposite sex, there is much to be learned from one another. Asking questions and sharing your personal needs will lead to a healthier love life.

WHAT MEN WANT

"It's absolutely unfair for women to say that guys only want one thing - sex. We also want food."
~ Jarod Kintz

"I don't know the question, but sex is definitely the answer."
~ Unknown Man

"Have no fear of perfection - you'll never reach it."
~ Salvador Dali

When asked to list everything he wanted from life, here's what one man had to say...

1. Sex
2. To play an instrument
3. A college education
4. A new surf board
5. 10 babies
6. A farm
7. A helicopter
8. An island
9. Sex with hot women
10. A woman who is independent, bold, thinkable, sexy, petite and strong. She has dark hair or blonde hair, salt and pepper, brown or red hair. She's comfortable with her hair, short or long, it doesn't matter. Boobs, A or B or C cup, any really as long as they are not saggy or too small. As for skin color it doesn't matter. Her height is preferably over 5'5 and under 6' I suppose but as for her face, she has just the right amount of make-up and is comfortable without make-up. She knows how to do her make-up. As for her smile, smile wrinkles are cool by me. She should have well-trimmed, nice nails that are not too long and beautiful well-manicured feet. She smells pretty or has no smell

and she should have nice teeth. Her teeth should be clean and straight. As for her ears, I'd just like them to be perfect and not stick out from her head too far. Hopefully she does not have fat earlobes. Her stomach is flat with smooth skin and her thighs are great. She has a nice ass that is rounded with smooth skin. A bubble butt in perfect shape is great. Her arms are lean but not too muscular and have no hanging skin. She has perfect fingers and lean, in-shape legs. She's smart, intellectual, and wealthy in her state of mind. A woman with money is nice, but more importantly she is active, adventuresome and an awesome mother. She's ageless. Her nose perfectly fits her face. She's not too hairy and has perfect eye brows that are well trimmed with no uni-brow. She definitely has a fun sense of adventure. She's not a partier but she does have hot girlfriends. All types of girlfriends are great. She loves only me and lets me have multiple girlfriends.

And the list of this man's desires went on...

11. A relationship where I don't want more sex outside the relationship
12. Enlightenment, brilliance
13. Math because it's logical, mystical and comprehensible
14. Time alone, time to do hobbies
15. A happy wife
16. A happy family
17. Success
18. Early retirement
19. To discover something great, write something great and change the world
20. Sex
21. A life that I can be the example of
22. To be financially free, with passive income with savings for my family and children. A pile of gold in

the basement and diamonds that I can shoot out of my slingshot.

23. Sex with two women at one time
24. As for my manhood I'd like to live a life without the effects of B.S., be myself, and stand up for what I believe in
25. To be educated and free thinking
26. To be a protector and a provider
27. I'd like some laziness with time for relaxing, recovering, meditating, nothingness and stillness
28. To have my vices in moderation and realize vices are just vices, but I'd love one ton of marijuana and be able to indulge with no lasting side-effects.
29. To have good health and be physically 31 years old always
30. As for toys I don't need excess baggage in life when the sun is free but I wouldn't mind some motorcycles, a guitar, a piano, a 4-wheel drive pick-up truck, a canoe and another surf board
31. I'd like to buy my wife a brand new BMW of her choice and buy my daughter the year of her birth sports car, take my truck to be restored and contract out for a new kitchen, bath and loft in my house plus add on another bathroom. I'd like the top of the line plasma 3D TV, a new blue ray player and tons of movies. I'd ensure my wife got her romantic comedies and I'd like all the Disney movies for my daughter. I'd love a new computer, a new laptop, a new cell phone and some other electronics. I'd like to buy my parents plane tickets to come see us and all the in-laws tickets as well. Would love a family vacation for all the family plus their salaries paid so they can get away.
32. Back to sex for a minute, I'd like for my wife to happily have sex with me anytime I wanted. 4a.m., 12a.m., 12p.m., 3p.m., just anytime I want.
33. Blow jobs are great but I'd rather have sex

34. Sex from the ceiling, on the floor, from behind on the couch, or in the doorway, sex on the sink, anywhere and anytime really

35. Porn fills the void of sex when I'm not getting it

36. Regarding, ex-girlfriends, I've been there done that, if the sex was good I'd take some more sex with exes but really prefer them to just be jealous. I would like to see that they are doing well but still dearly miss me. Want them to be jealous of my wife and child and realize they could have had this too.

37. I'd like some nothingness, need plenty of time for nothingness ideally

38. Also just love to go for a run, go to the beach check out the surf and mountains and hike the ridge line

39. Hot sex

40. Any adventure is good including hiking, mountain biking, camping, volleyball, softball, soccer, white water rafting, a voyage or a trek, etc.

41. Regarding guys time, I would love to do poker night, drink some beer and restore an old car

42. Regarding other girls, I like going to the beach, hanging out and talking with them, girls in bikinis or in a hot tub, making out and sex with them or course

43. When I see hot older women I think, "wow" I'm impressed that she takes care of herself and I hope my wife looks that good when she's that old

44. I'm not a fan of politics

45. Work is good and provides discipline

46. Regarding having to go to a job to make money, that's rough. I don't want that!

47. I want the option to help friends and give. I do want to do that!

48. Finally, I'd like to change the world and leave a lasting positive impression. Oh and did I mention sex?

You can see this man is pretty easy to figure out. He simply wants it ALL! So if most men want it all, you can see how this simplifies things. Think about it. Most men will never be completely satisfied with just one woman as they still want all the other women as well. They want sex every way they can get it anytime they want it. They can take or leave exes most of the time (so don't get caught up on the exes ladies!). They want money and power, peace and freedom, a committed partner who pampers them and well everything perfectly the way they want it. Now that you know this, you can let go of all the stress about losing your man to another woman. Why? Well because he'd still want all the same things if he was with her too. So who better than you to do the job?!

You've heard the saying with regards to some of the famous hot super models and actors out there... "Somebody's tired of fucking that!" Ladies, it's true. How many hot actors or actresses have been cheated on or left and everyone was in shock. Well, there's no shock in my opinion. Men want it all. So if you don't do the best possible job of providing that for them, they have the potential to cheat or quit. Do not let this discourage you. You are at no less advantage than anyone else. In fact, because you have taken an interest in what you can do, you are at an advantage. That being said, let's focus on what you can do to please your man. Some of the results will relate to what type of integrity your chosen man has. Let's look at truly what you can do.

Work with what you have in your control and ladies, this is simple. Don't complicate this or you will bypass your own effectiveness.

How to simply give your man everything he wants...

1. If you're in a fully committed and already sexual relationship, give him all the sex he wants.
2. Be secure with yourself.
3. No matter what you look like, feel great about yourself. Men will respond to energy far more

41

powerfully than to what they see. Think about a time when a man you knew was attracted to or in love with a woman where you couldn't understand the attraction. Likely it was because the girl was so secure with herself that she exuded sex appeal.

4. Be sexy. It's just a state of mind.
5. Be trusting. The alternative is pointless.
6. Help your man to feel secure about your loyalty but maintain an element of mystery.
7. Dote on your man from a confident place. Give him tons of consistent praise about his masculinity. He needs it. This will help fulfill some of his need for power. Balance this though with your own independence.
8. Give your man time to himself. When he needs it, give it to him and do not give him shit about it.
9. Be an amazing mother if you are a parent or pregnant.
10. Shave your legs, do your make up appropriately and dress well for your body type.
11. Smile!
12. Smile!
13. Smile!
14. Be grateful. Count your blessings and acknowledge how good you have it. Gratitude for what you have always brings more good in the areas of your life where you are grateful.

That's it! There's nothing more you can do and nothing more that you need to do. Trying to address anything that is not within your control is pure silliness. You cannot for example control the fact that your man is a man and therefore programmed differently than you. You cannot prevent the existence of other women on the planet. And you cannot be perfect as there is truly no such thing. So be yourself and tap into your own sex appeal. Exude the confidence of someone who knows that they are lucky and therefore so is your partner.

Be at peace with being in your own skin. Love your own body. Take care of yourself. And trust that everything else falls into place.

INSIGHTS

Cake and Eat It Too

1. Everyone wants to have their cake and to eat it too. Yes, it's true what all men want. Men want to marry their queen. Men also want hot sex with beautiful women.
2. Today's society says women win. In most cases, men have to compromise on the hot sex with other women desire if they want to settle down or have a healthy marriage.
3. Women know exactly what they want and are willing to go after it.
4. Willpower leads to power.
5. Hinting to a guy is futile. Men do not possess the "Hint" gene.
6. The only effective way to communicate your needs to a man is to spell them out for him.
7. Men should be allowed to make mistakes without constant instruction, at least some of the time.
8. Dependence is unhealthy.
9. Sexual prowess should be developed.

Obvious Choices

1. Walk away from a relationship with someone who is not looking for one.
2. Stop now if you have started down the path with a man who tells you he does not want kids, if you are hoping to have children.
3. Do not expect a person in a long-term relationship with another partner to leave that person for you.
4. Choose a partner with habits you can tolerate.
5. Choose a partner within a reasonable proximity of yourself.
6. Be willing to walk away before you arrive.

7. Women sometimes lie about orgasms. Go with it.
8. Don't be too anxious. Be confident and let others call you.
9. A guy who exudes crazy levels of confidence (not arrogance) can be hot to almost any woman.

The Recurring Theme

1. Generally speaking, women are more emotional than men.
2. Men tend to be at first more visual and sexual than women.
3. There are variations with both sexes where some men are more emotional and some women are more sexual.
4. Feeling love leads women to own their sexuality.
5. Getting hot sex leads men to give more love.
6. Both love and sex beget each other.
7. Both sexes should practice becoming professionals at the parts they need to play to get what they each most desire in return.
8. Men should play the part of the nurturing, loving, gentle guy who dotes on and adores his woman while still maintaining his protective and confident masculine side.
9. Women should play the part of the sensual sexual desiring woman who can't live without her man's penis.
10. With women sometimes the issue is the need for more love and cuddling while other times the issue is in fact the quality of sex.
11. Men want women to want them so much that they beg for it. Women want men to adore, love, compliment, cuddle and tease them before sex.
12. It is up to each of us to take responsibility for taking the initiative to give our partner what they need.
13. No one is a mind reader. The most likely way to get what you need is to spell it out for each other. Giving

your partner details will help them understand how you are programmed.

What Men Want

1. Men are simple. They just want it all!
2. Men can take or leave exes most of the time.
3. Most straight men at least secretly want hot sex with a variety of hot women.
4. Assuming you're a woman, you have equally as much opportunity to please your man as any other woman.
5. There are simple steps a woman can take to please a man, including giving him all the sex he wants (assuming the woman is in an already committed sexual relationship), owning her own sexuality, and being confident in her own skin. Also, it is important to both praise a man and allow him time to himself when he needs it. Smile and be grateful for what you have.
6. Women need to own their own sexuality and trust that when they are comfortable in their own skin and grateful for what they have, all the rest falls into place.

2

All's Fair in Love and War

POWER, MOSTLY FOR THE LADIES

*"Personal power is the ability to stand on your own two feet,
with a smile on your face, in the middle of a universe
that contains a million ways to crush you."*
~ J.Z. Colby, Nebador

*"He who controls others may be powerful, but he who
has mastered himself is mightier still."*
~ Lao-Tzu

"What is he STUPID?!" If I had a dollar for every time I heard that question, I'd be a wealthy woman. That exact question usually comes from a girl soon after a recent long drawn out commentary about how that same guy was so amazing that she was sure that he was the only guy in the world for her. Typically, I'd also just heard from the same woman how she had never met any other guy in her entire life who made her feel the way this one made her feel. Then out of the blue the guy did something "yet again" to piss her off.

Ladies, most men can be a bit dense when it comes to women at times. If you are a smart, witty and independent woman this will be especially true. Let me break it down. This is what happens. Men can spot a GREAT girl a mile away. Watch out as guys have been trained by the movies to get the girl! They know how to persist. They know how to make adjustments to their approach and strategy when needed. I could probably write an entire book just on how guys are trained by the movies. However, not to worry because once women actually realize it, they'll see just how much power they actually have.

Guys love women who are oozing confidence and sex appeal. It's true ladies, sex appeal from the core of their being. Sexuality does not come from sleaziness or from faking sexy by the clothes that are worn. It means confidence and beauty from the inside out. Let me give you an example. You know that time some guy you loved way too much, devastated your world just one too many times, and you finally got so pissed off that you screamed "Fuuuuuuuuuuck him!!! What, is he stupid?!!!" One of those moments when you were decidedly grounded and you made up your mind you didn't care any more about what he thought. You were going to stand up straight and channel your energy into making yourself the hottest girl who ever crossed his path and he was never going to get you back. That's the kind of oozing sexuality I'm talking about here.

You know that sex appeal that those certain women have, that when they pass by your man, you wish you could have tripped them? Your first jealous reaction is to tell your man that she wasn't even that pretty. But he thought differently. I'm talking about the type of sexuality that drives men wild. You know the powerful actresses who seriously make you jealous? That's the kind of sexuality I'm talking about. And you know that person you really are on the inside if he'd just realized it?

That's the kind of sexuality I'm talking about. I'm talking about the kind of sexuality that radiates out of your being without even having to be in a guy's presence for him to feel it. We all have it. It's about tapping into that sexual energy to make your man want you.

Assuming you have not already slept with the guy in this case, or assuming you are broken up, here's the BIG SECRET to really owning it with a man. DRUM ROLL PLEASE... WITHHOLD THE SEX! Again ladies, the secret is to simply WITHHOLD IT! Let the energy radiate from you without words. You do NOT need to give up your body to prove anything! This is the kind of confidence and sexuality that you do not have to tell your man about or substantiate in any way, shape or form. You do not have to point it out. You can let your man think everything is all right and he can mess up all day long and you do not need to say one word because you know at the end of the day, you and only you, own your sexy self. You just let this sexuality speak for itself. You decide when and where to draw the line. You're so confident that it does not matter what he does. You don't care one iota what your man does because you are so sexy, in control and sizzling hot from the inside out you can literally write your ticket for anything you choose to do. You're the fucking prize!!! Not him! (Side note: If you are a guy who is struggling to get a girl, this section applies to you too. Just reverse those roles!) Power comes from a deep place. You merely need to tap into it, as it is always there.

A tip on power: As you tap into your own power, strangers and others will notice way before the person you are trying to impress. To help you retain your power, keep it to yourself when you receive compliments from others. Especially those compliments or comments you receive from the opposite sex. The more you tap into this power the more others will notice you and let you know about it. The immediate urge will be to tell the person you are most infatuated by, all about the attention you are getting from others. The key here is to let them see it without ever saying one word about it. When others compliment you, take it in and allow it to further energize your powerful state of being. Compliments will continue coming. Do not be fooled into thinking you need to make your partner jealous by sharing what you've heard from others. It's only a matter of time before they will witness it. The compliments will never run dry. Let those comments and actions from others fuel your power without talking about it. There is never a need to share the details of the attention you get from others to substantiate yourself. Just take compliments and comments in and let them live inside you! The sexiest people alive do not go around telling people that someone whistled at them or commented about how great they looked. They just live it.

ME, ME, ME

"Humility is not thinking less of yourself, it's thinking of yourself less."
~ *C.S. Lewis*

What do all people have in common? It's all about them. It's just the way our lives work.

Most human beings feel similar human emotions. That includes the people you love, people who love you, people you know, and people you don't know. People all feel. People feel love, joy, pain, hurt, frustration, anger, excitement, sexy, ugly, good, bad, relaxed, scared, alone, overwhelmed, peaceful, high, low, numb, nothing and everything. We often get wrapped up in our own worlds to such a degree that we forget that the people we want something from also have things in their lives that are going on that are equally important to them. Being selfless means to live as you expect to live, not to ask others to do the very same.

What if others suddenly stepped outside of themselves for a moment each day to consider you? How would that make you feel? People in line at the grocery store for example. Or people at the drive-through. People on the road and people at home.

What if you went out into the world today and were more considerate of every person you crossed paths with and it created a ripple effect that caused them to be even just a bit more aware or conscious of others. It doesn't take much to shock people with consideration these days. My husband and I have been paying for the meals for the people behind us, when we go through select drive-thrus for years. Same with tolls and parking. We love to make people smile. Often we pay for random meals or drinks for people in restaurants if we see someone who looks unhappy and we want to cheer them up. Other times we do it because they look happy and we want to add to their experience. Sometimes, however, we forget to do it for each other.

It is a joy to brighten anyone's day and especially your partner's, even if just for a moment. A moment for some lasts all day, a week or a simple act of consideration can actually impact someone for a lifetime. Take for example the impact of a simple decision from one moment ago in my life. My husband is playing a video game on his iPad as I type. It is 6:49a.m. and he decides he wants to tell me about this game and how these coins get in the way when he attempts to run 100 yards (as an animated character), which I'm really not clear how you gauge on an iPad. As you can imagine it does take some level of concentration to write a book. However, given the timing of the topic I happen to be writing about, and though secretly annoyed by his talking to me about his irritating game, I decided to stop and really listen to him and take an interest in what he was describing. You should have seen the unbelievable excitement he expressed when I showed an interest and the laughter that it lead to because I truly decided to be conscientious of what was temporarily important to him. My instinct was to say, "Babe, can't you see I'm writing a book here? Really? Do you have to tell me about your time-wasting video game?" Instead I stopped and listened and because I did, it made all the difference.

All people get caught up. No matter how important our

lives are to us, others' lives are more important to them than our own. When you stop and consider your significant other you change your relationship for the better and you change your own personal experience with how you relate to other people as well. Taking that same principal of consideration into the bedroom can also greatly improve your love life! When others consider you first, be sure to spell out your appreciation for them so that they want to do it again.

PLENTY OF FISH IN THE SEA - GETTING THE UPPER HAND

"There are plenty of fish in the sea."
~ *American Proverb*

Whether you're a man or a woman, the first step in getting the upper hand in an unbalanced relationship is to realize that there are a billion other people who you could potentially connect with if you open your heart to the possibility. Whether you are sure you must have a particular person or you are ready to open your eyes to connecting with new people, people are abundant. People are attracted to self-assuredness in other people. In order to get the upper hand with anyone, a person must start by seeing the big picture. My sister and I have always said to our friends and each other when feeling a loss of control in a relationship, "You will have this person or somebody better." No one person is your only option in life. Not even if you're married. If it doesn't work out with one person there sincerely will be another opportunity to fall madly in-love with someone else. Nobody ever believes this while they are feeling heartbroken. It is however, true!

Let's talk about getting the upper hand. When you are groveling or chasing after someone and they are not responding, there are some fundamental things that are usually taking place. Once the pitfalls are identified, you can usually better play the game that is necessary to get the upper hand.

Let's look at five basic ideas which are worth considering when you're trying to bring balance in a relationship.

Five Rules/Tips for increasing your attractiveness...

1. <u>Be mysterious</u>. Human beings love mystery. Keep the details of your personal feelings to yourself. People who are groveling or trying too hard to get another person to love them are usually too willing to quickly spell out their undying love for the person they are crazy about. This takes away the mystery and immediately gives the other person the complete upper hand. If you have already done this, it is OK. We've all done it. Just stop. Don't do it again.

2. <u>Give the other person space</u>. Space creates natural curiosity and attraction. Stop worrying about whether or not you will lose this person if you give them space. In most cases, especially when it comes to a man's needs, space will create desire and longing that does not happen when you are constantly together.

3. <u>Hide your jealousy</u>. If you are jealous of something or someone, ACT like you are not. Fake it until you make it a reality and remember that there is no other YOU on earth. You are unique and not in competition with others for someone's love. Be willing to allow the person you love to go be with whatever or whoever it is you are jealous of. Let them be free. Freedom to choose and freedom to be is what life is about. You do not want someone who is with you because they are being forced or being guilt tripped into being with you. You want this person to be with you by choice. Let them go explore whatever it is they are seeking and allow them to come to you by free will. There are healthy ways to gain strength during jealous moments.

4. <u>Find your independence</u>. Even if you are depressed, do something that takes your mind partially off of your

neediness. Neediness is unattractive to all of us. If you are feeling needy, channel it. Donate some of your time to helping feed the homeless. Help out at a shelter. Do something to remind yourself how much you have to give and how little you need compared to other people less fortunate. Take your mind off your moping and give.

5. <u>Get yourself in shape</u>. Channeling your energy into things that make you feel good or release adrenalin are extremely helpful in gaining self-control. Consider the gym, a run, a good physical class, a massage or any other physical outlet. This will help you to get into the now by feeling your own body. Feeling your own body grounds you in the moment where you can for even a second realize that you are OK! And you are going to feel great again! Do this and you will begin to get your emotional strength back. Be proactive and seek to better your emotional state through your physical state which you can control. Meditate and breathe.

Those things which are the hardest to do are the most rewarding in the end. Sometimes simply trusting that you are not going to lose anything that is truly meant to be yours, can be the most difficult concept to accept. Faith in your own self-worth can be quite difficult when your heart is hurting. Yet you will attract to you that which you dwell upon for better or for worse. Trust in positive possibilities as you choose your thoughts. Allowing someone to have their space does not risk anything. In fact it only gives way for the magnetic attraction that will follow if you allow it.

FINE LINE BETWEEN TURN-ON AND TURN-OFF

"People call me John, but you can call me tonight!"
~ Unknown

"You must be tired.
Because you've been running through my head all day."
~ Unknown

"Do you believe in love at first sight, or should I walk by again?"
~ Unknown

There's a fine line between a turn-on and a turn-off. Ladies especially know what I'm talking about if you've ever been with a guy who was whispering the sweetest words and then suddenly he threw in something that was corny or sexually crude that made you cringe. The guy probably had good intentions. He was just operating with what he knew best and assumed that what might turn him on, would turn you on. Not often the case! On the other hand, sometimes the most intense sexual comments can be hot if said appropriately timed. The same is true for both sexes only in opposite ways. A guy hearing a girl say sweet words can be nice at times but too much of it is a major turn-off. In many cases, a guy in fact will be more likely to fall for a girl who talks dirty to him. Although again, too much or ill-timed dirty talk can take away the sweetness of a girl. A guy often wants a girl who seems innocent on some level but knows all the sexy hot bedroom tricks. We've all heard about the men, who fantasize about the librarian who's a maniac in the bedroom. Let's face it, men and women are different creatures.

Here's where women tend to miss the mark. Women often know how to play the game in the very beginning of a relationship and tend to exude confidence and sensuality instinctively. A guy then in response to his attraction starts saying the nicest things and a girl falls hard for his appropriate use of kind words in reply to her sexual energy. Once the girl falls, she too quickly begins expressing her feelings mistakenly thinking that he would like to hear all the details of her emotional thoughts. After all he was sharing loving words with her. Unfortunately, there's a disconnect. The guy more than likely understood that the woman wanted to hear loving words and he used this to his advantage to get what he wanted which was actually sexual in nature. Now this hot sexy babe he was beginning to fall for starts describing in detail her every emotional thought and replaces her sexual energy with cuddling and emotional neediness which completely turns him off. The woman then feels him retreating and in a panic exhibits more feeling behavior in an attempt to get reassurance causing the guy to pull-back even further. Then if she's a smart woman with some self-control, she will realize what's happening and she herself will muster up the energy to pull-back from the guy. This allows him the space he needs to say to himself, "Hey wait a minute, where's she going?" Then he'll come back right as she is thinking "forget him" and he'll say more kind words. His return will then cause the girl to unknowingly relax yet again and respond with overly sentimental words. If the woman continues down this path, he'll pull-back, pull-back, then turn and run. Remember what he actually was attracted to was her confidence and unspoken sensuality or the type of female energy that really makes him feel like a man.

A woman grows fonder of a man with more time spent with him whereas a guy often needs time <u>away</u> from a woman to grow more affectionate. This natural occurrence can be a positive experience if it is understood. If you're a woman, you've noticed how men pull away. At some point it is inevitable that you are trying to figure out what the heck they are thinking. This is usually the precise time when they wouldn't tell you what was on their mind if you begged them on your knees to say what they were thinking. The reality is, they may just truly need some time to themselves to deal with whatever it is that they need to think about or <u>not</u> think about as is often the case I'm told by men. They need this space to build up or replenish their testosterone levels. This is not a bad thing. It is completely normal.

If you can stand to be in a healthy relationship without pushing your personal needs on your partner, this back and forth thing that happens between men and women can become simple and easy to accept. Let's talk about women for a moment. We grow closer to men when they spend intimate time with us. Yet when we are away, we gain our independence. When we get some alone time and we aren't groveling for a guy's attention, we become stronger as women. We need this as much as we need the intimacy. This is why it's great to have hobbies that occupy our time during those times when a man needs his space. As one friend of a friend once spelled it out for me, "To keep a guy happy, it's simple. Feed 'em, fuck 'em and leave 'em the fuck alone." There may be a lot of truth in that statement.

Unlike with a man, a woman will often withdraw or pull-back a little from an intense come-back after a man has had his alone time. We ladies say to ourselves, "Are you kidding me?! I've been wanting your attention for X days/weeks/etc. and now, finally right when I don't give a shit any longer, here you are!" We then need to be wined and dined to warm back up. If you're a man and were wondering why you were receiving a cold reception whenever you came back ready for some love, after being in your man cave for a period of time, now you know why. Ladies need to be warmed up and then we will give you a reception you could only dream of. If you forget the warmer, you can forget the warm reception.

What's right for one person is not always right for another. This is especially true between the sexes. Keeping an open mind to the possibility that your process may differ from another person's process is a sure way to remain flexible. Remaining flexible allows you to grow and discover what works for the person you love.

INSIGHTS

Power, Mostly for the Ladies •

1. All men can be dense when it comes to women from time to time.
2. Women have a tremendous amount of power if only they realize it.
3. Guys love women who are sexy and confident from the inside out.
4. Channel your sexuality and withhold the goods. Do not prove your sexuality by giving up your body freely.
5. Once you've made personal changes, be patient until your partner notices the new you. You do not need to speak of it in any way. Just allow it to show organically.
6. There is no need to tell your partner about the compliments you receive from others of the opposite sex in an attempt to make them jealous. Just take in compliments and let them live inside you powering your natural sensuality which will shine through without your acknowledgment.

Me, Me, Me

1. All people feel love, joy, pain, hurt, frustration, anger, excitement, sexy, ugly, good, bad, relaxed, scared, alone, overwhelmed, peaceful, high, low, numb, nothing and everything.
2. People tend to get wrapped up in their own worlds forgetting that others are also absorbed by their own worlds.
3. Being selfless means to live as you expect to live but not to demand the same from others.
4. Taking just a moment to consider another person's perspective can change a life.
5. When you consider your significant other and their needs first, you can often greatly improve your

relationship.
6. Take consideration to bed with you and you may greatly improve your love life.

Plenty of Fish in the Sea - Getting the Upper Hand

1. There really are plenty of fish in the sea.
2. You will have this person or someone better.
3. The things that are sometimes the hardest to do are usually the most rewarding in the end.
4. Be mysterious. Human beings love mystery. Keep the details of your personal feelings to yourself.
5. Give others their space. Space creates natural curiosity and attraction.
6. Hide jealousy. If you are jealous of something or someone, ACT like you are not. Fake it 'til you make it a reality and remember that there is no other you on earth.
7. Find your independence if you get down or depressed. Take your mind off your moping by helping others.
8. Get in shape. Be proactive with that which is within your control and seek to better your emotional state through your physical state.

Fine Line between Turn-on and Turn-off

1. Men and women are different. What turns on a woman is different from what turns on a man.
2. Use self-control when speaking to the opposite sex. Mushy overly gooey words do not turn-on a man. Whereas too crass of sexual words can often turn-off a woman.
3. A woman grows fonder of a man with more time spent with him, whereas, a guy usually needs more time away from a woman to want her more.
4. Men need to learn to take it slow after time away from a woman. Women need to be warmed up gently.

3

A Date, A Kiss

A SINGLE DATE

"Be yourself; everyone else is already taken."
~ Oscar Wilde

"To be yourself in a world that is constantly trying to make you something else is the greatest accomplishment."
~ Ralph Waldo Emerson

Some people love dating while others abhor it. Regardless of your stance on dating, you clearly have a reason if you are doing it. Regardless of your reason, if you're doing it, every date should be treated as if it will be the last date you will ever go on whether you like the person or not. This tiny piece of advice if taken to heart can sincerely change your life, let alone your dating.

How do you act when you are on a date? Are you

completely yourself or do you try to impress the other person? Do you ask questions or do you do all the talking? Do you put all your energy on the other person without regard for how they view you? Are you fearful or fearless? Do you treat them with respect but open up without worry about their judgment?

As with every interview, every audition, every first date and every repetitive date, if even with the same person after 5, 10 or 20 years, the greatest gift you can offer another person is your true self. The more you open up your heart, the more you will offer the world. Ask yourself if you were to never have an opportunity at a second date with this person and this was the only time you would ever get to be with this person for the rest of your life, how would you truly act. Let's take it one step further. If you knew that after your date, this person would be hit by a bus and killed, how would you behave? Keeping in mind that this other person is a human being like you with fears, joys, love, worry, etc., and of course assuming your gut instincts don't tell you that they are toxic in some way, how would you behave if you only had a short amount of time with this person? Not every date will be with "the one" but every date is a chance to connect with another human being who will be forever changed by their encounter with you. Hard to believe one person has all that power, but it's true. You can actually change someone's life as well as your own, each time you connect by simply remaining open to the possibility.

In order to make an impact on another person in a way that can change their life, you only need to be yourself. Channeling your own inner beauty can make for a great time. Showing up as yourself takes away all the pressure to impress and allows people to connect with you. You cannot control this in others, but naturally when you are relaxed, it relaxes those around you. A word of caution: If you have not practiced being completely yourself prior to now, it is a good idea to take precautions to draw your own boundaries. If you open up to another person, they will likely be quite attracted to your energy since so few people have a tendency to do this. Therefore, if you do not want a person to kiss you for example, you may need to say that. There are two paths you can go when connecting with someone who is attracted to you. Open up further. Or guard yourself. What I'm suggesting is, rather than guarding yourself, open up further while being up front about your intentions and boundaries. If you are worried about what actions a person might take while they are feeling an unusual level of ease or comfort with you, be up front about where your boundaries lie. This way you can continue to be true to your nature without having to put up the walls that are sometimes necessary to keep a person at arm's length.

There are always new opportunities to become more authentic in life. This is especially exciting when dating. Some people have mastered dating. Maybe you're one of them. A master dater knows how to channel their best qualities, be true to themselves and simultaneously play a subtle game of cat and mouse with the person they are on a date with. If you are trying to increase the interest level of the other party, mystery and intrigue are a part of the interweave necessary during a date. At the end of the day, dating usually indicates first or initial encounters with potential partners. What could be more fun than living out that life truthfully by bringing your real self along? When it comes to matching up long term, the greatest gift you can give yourself is trust in the end result, knowing that it will always be in your best interest. Freedom to date without the need to manipulate fate allows everyone to have a great time while you get to know others as well as yourself better.

ONE KISS CAN LAST A LIFETIME

"A man's kiss is his signature."
~ *Mae West*

Most women can kiss. They have soft lips and allow you to want more as you touch them. They use their tongue selectively and sweetly. They are not forceful and they are willing to put their mouth ever so close and exchange air without touching. A simple exchange of breath. A touch without force. A touch without touching. A willingness to surrender to another person's intimacy while holding back ever so slightly. Kissing can be the most powerful thing in the universe if given and received properly. However, a kiss with force will destroy all fantasies if not done with the appropriate passion. A kiss requires extreme control but can simultaneously be done with complete surrender. It can be tantric.

Most of us have heard the advice "90/10." Meaning the guy should go 90% and let the lady come the other 10%. It's true most of the time. Let us want you so much that we come to you. Do not push yourself on us or we may retreat; maybe not physically but definitely emotionally.

A single kiss can last a lifetime. When you close your eyes and let your mouth touch another person's mouth, suddenly it does not matter who they are or what they look like if only they can kiss. What I'd do to kiss a great kisser at any point in my life. A kiss can sustain a person for years. The thought of a great kiss literally can stay with someone and keep them loving or longing forever. I personally cannot live without kissing. The longer I go without a good kiss the more I long for the intimacy, at times without regard nearly for whom it is from. Sometimes, I just need to kiss.

So the key is this. If you are going to kiss someone, open your soul. Let energy speak for itself and allow breath to be exchanged. Never push and always receive. Try connecting without touching. Let it last. Put your attention on the other person and respond to them. Stop thinking about it. Just be with it and experience it fully.

INSIGHTS

<u>A Single Date</u>

1. Each date should be treated as if it may be your last.
2. The greatest gift you can offer another person is yourself.
3. The more you open up your heart, the more you will offer the world.
4. Every date is a chance to relate to someone who will be forever changed by their encounter with you.
5. Showing up as yourself takes away all the pressure to impress and allows people to connect with you.
6. Put your boundaries on the table if you are worried about what actions a person might take while they are feeling a refreshing level of ease or comfort with you.
7. Remember that intrigue creates attraction.
8. Be true to yourself.

<u>One Kiss can last a Lifetime</u>

1. Guys should go 90% and let the ladies come the other 10%.
2. Hold back. Do <u>not</u> push yourself on another person.
3. Kiss with an open soul.
4. Let energy speak for itself and allow breath to be exchanged.
5. Open up to receive.
6. Connect without touching.
7. If you're a man, let a woman want you so much that she comes to you.
8. Let it last. Don't rush it.
9. Put your attention on the other person and respond to them.
10. Stop thinking about it. Be in the moment.

4

Marriage - Why Me?

UNDERSTANDING MEN'S DISINTEREST

"I want my time to be taken up by chores, errands, appointments and arguments. In other words, I want to get married."
~ Jarod Kintz, I Want

"By all means marry;
if you get a good wife, you'll become happy;
if you get a bad one, you'll become a philosopher."
~ Socrates

"Marriage is neither heaven nor hell, it is simply purgatory."
~ Abraham Lincoln

"The secret of a happy marriage remains a secret."
~ Henny Youngman

"I was married by a judge. I should have asked for a jury."
~ Groucho Marx

*"Married men live longer than single men, but married men are
a lot more willing to die."*
~ Johnny Carson

"Marriage is a blast! Like a bomb."
~ Julieanne-ism

Ladies, understanding men's disinterest in marriage is quite
straight forward if you just pay attention to what everyone's
saying about it. First and foremost, it is not personal! Most men
are desperately afraid of a marriage commitment. Why?
Probably for lots of reasons, many of which have to do with
what they've witnessed in everyone else's marriages such as
decreased sex, boredom, accountability to a woman other than
their mother, the idea of being nagged or told what to do, kids,
financial loss, loss of freedom and well let's face it, the thought
of being limited to sex with just one woman for the rest of their
lives. I know us ladies don't want to hear that but let's just
address the reality for a quick moment and then move on to
what we can do about it.

Men have no problem with love and definitely wish they
could find satisfaction in true love with just one woman.
Unfortunately, the thought of giving up their freedom in any
area of their life is not something they relish. Understand this is
true for the species. It is not unique to one guy and you cannot
change this about men! So concede that it is what it is and let it
go. It just is.

In order to persuade your man to marry you if you have
found "the one" and he is dragging his feet, here is my simple
advice. Give him this book and highlight what applies, so that
he better understands a woman's desire for the Fairy Tale. Or
spell it out for him (without emotion) and inform him that
marriage is a deep desire of yours and that if he doesn't handle

it, he risks the possibility of someday losing you to a man who can. However, tread lightly such that you are communicating this to impress upon him the deep importance of the subject for you personally without actually threatening him. That's it. Spell it out and stop playing the game for a moment to do it. Then let it go and do not mention it again. Either he gets it or he doesn't. Let him take the risk! And hopefully he'll step up to the plate!

Men's Fears about Marriage:

1. One woman for the rest of their lives
2. Decrease in sex (The stories they hear from other married men)
3. Discovering who a woman really is after marriage (The woman not revealing her true self prior to marriage)
4. Women letting themselves go after marriage (Getting lazy, cranky, unhappy, etc.)
5. Women's nagging
6. Loss of passion
7. Women trying to change the men
8. Financial woes
9. Loss of control of possessions
10. Sharing everything
11. Loss of freedom
12. Loss of excitement and adventure
13. Not together long enough
14. Societal judgments
15. Family judgments
16. Age differences
17. Too young
18. Already been married
19. Afraid to mess up an already good thing
20. Afraid of the answer
21. Got to save money to get a ring
22. Pressure about how to propose

23. Questioning if someone is the ideal mate
24. Not thinking a woman really wants to be married
25. Losing half if it ends in divorce
26. Fear from seeing parent's relationships end in divorce
27. Taking on the woman's debt
28. What if's? What if the grass is greener?
29. Fear of being pressured to have children
30. In-laws

And the list goes on!

Let's face it, marriage is not easy. Moreover, marriage clearly does not eliminate problems nor does any married couple maintain the exact same initial spark and passion forever more. Things do change. Women are less likely to admit this than men, while men analyze it thoroughly prior to proposing. Men's analysis of the obvious parallels between relationship issues and marriage often lead them to stall their actions of a proposal. Men simply tend to be more realistic about the realities of changes to come and yet at the same time that very analysis often leads them to paralysis. If a woman wants to sincerely ease her man on this subject, she'd likely be better off to validate his fears by admitting that nothing stays the same forever but then reassure him about the adventure of life's journey. The only way to prove to a man that marriage can be a great thing, is to live it once you are married. Once married, couples should be transparent about their needs while they simultaneously consider their partner's needs regularly.

There is no magic cure for men's marriage paralysis. However, men do eventually settle down in most cases. Faithful or not, men do their best to please their women if they truly love them. Accepting that men have a fear of marriage and that they simply look at it differently than women is the simplest way to come to terms with yet another very normal difference between men and women. Coming to terms about these fundamental differences allows for better understanding and all around fewer hurt feelings between the sexes. If something such as marriage is eating at you or making you resentful whether you're a man or a woman, it is a very good idea to spell it out for your partner so that they understand your views on the topic.

WOMEN'S DESIRE FOR THE FAIRY TALE

"If I'm honest I have to tell you I still read fairy-tales
and I like them best of all."
~ *Audrey Hepburn*

Understanding women's desire for the "fairy tale" wedding and understanding men's lack of interest can seem as unclear as men and women in general. Ladies already understand their point of view on this topic. This section is dedicated to unmarried men who on a serious note think that they might like to keep their woman happy and for men who have decided that they are with "the one" or "a keeper."

Most ladies deep down have a secret desire to have the fairy tale day when they marry the person that they are passionately in love with. The key here is "passionately." They want this day to happen while they are in an exciting phase of their relationship. Not after the passion has subsided, but while it's hot and heavy. There's a reason why in the movies, women get married while it's incredibly intense.

The bottom line is that if you are a man who adores your woman, you should ask her to marry you while there is desire. Do not wait until your relationship is stagnant or until your woman is pleading with you for an engagement, or worse yet, asking you to marry her. Once you are at that point you will have a much more difficult time being "the man" throughout the remainder of your relationship. Screw concerns about divorce. The great thing is, if you end up absolutely needing to get a divorce, you can. Stop worrying about the future. No one ever knows what the future holds.

On a side note: Whether you've been married before or not,

waited for a long time or not, and whether or not there is passion at this time in your relationship, be sure to open the lines of communication regarding marriage.

A "fairy tale" wedding does not necessarily denote a "fancy" wedding. Many women would elope in the passion phase of a relationship if it just meant that they could be with the person they love. Most women DO in fact want to marry the partner of their dreams but often start out acting like they are the no-pressure sexy hot babe you always dreamed about who doesn't even think about marriage. Once we've matured enough to catch on to men's disinterest in marriage we strategically deny our desires for the fairy tale wedding to convince a guy that we were made for them. I assure you it is a secret manipulation in an attempt to convince the guy to change his view on the subject.

Let me give you a couple of examples of things that ladies might say that do not really mean what they say... 1) "It's like we are already married anyway." *Definition: "I really wish we were married by now. I cannot believe I can't PROVE our love to the world."* 2) "I don't need to get married, as long as I'm with you." *Definition: "You better ask me to marry you fool, without me having to spell it out for you."*

Stalling a woman who has made up her mind that you're the one for her, will work for a minute but eventually it will lead a woman to frustration. The woman wants confirmation from her man while she's in ecstasy. To a woman, a man willing to propose while still passionate in a relationship, without over analysis of the topic, is a man who a woman would call a "REAL MAN!" Proposing in a timely fashion gives a man tremendous leverage later on in a marriage.

I understand the hesitancy to propose to a woman when our society has an increasingly high rate of divorce, exceeding 50%. I attribute a small part of this to men's lack of willingness to propose at the right time. Back in the day, a man had to be married to a woman before he could sleep with her. The tendency was that proposals happened much more quickly than they do in modern times. That should also give women some indication as to the power they have by withholding sex in the beginning of a relationship.

If you're a man who has held on to a lady for years and years already without asking her to marry you, I urge you to shock her and PROPOSE ALREADY. Drop the excuses! Buy a lab grown diamond if you have to. A quick side-note on that: Man-made diamonds are affordable, perfect quality and test as genuine diamonds. They have even perfected the "imperfection" that all diamonds have. If you do plan to buy a man-made or lab grown diamond, make sure that your lady first sees the film *Blood Diamond* and that she is on the same page with you about this subject.

You can plan the wedding after the proposal which is a huge part of the fun for the ladies so there is no need to dwell on the details. You can also actually propose without a ring and allow her to design it or pick it out. If you are concerned about verifying if this is the right girl for you, yet you are going to propose anyway, be sure to set your wedding date out a while.

Note of caution for the men: If you are suspect that your woman is not that in to you, please disregard the advice given in this section and do NOT rush a proposal. This section is specifically for men who know without question that they are with a woman that they cannot imagine life without and she is a woman who has clearly expressed the same feelings. There is no magic amount of time that you have to be together, however keep in mind that some very predictable things happen during the first three to six months and again around a year into a relationship. For example, people tend to be in a blissful state during the first three months having the time of their lives. Analysis and the act of tremendous balancing happens anywhere between four to six months. Often between six and seven months, one person or the other panics a bit and overcompensates by coming on too strong therefore pushing the other person away. Or one or the other person decides that they are not that into the other person after all. This is natural.

It's the time when people decide whether or not they are interested in getting to know the other person better. A lot of insight comes between this time and the year marker. And at a year or slightly after, things begin to settle in and you will have to address the person with slightly less intense hormonal and chemical releases. Therefore, it may be a good idea in many cases, to hold off on an actual wedding date until you get past some of these common stages.

That said, there are exceptions to all rules and there are certainly people who meet, fall in love and get married within weeks and it lasts forever. There are also stories of people who stay together for twenty years and then get married and immediately end up divorced. Trust your gut and do what feels right. Never force something that is not organic. Marriage will not keep someone in your life if you are not meant to be. So never propose for ownership. Proposals should be reserved for romantic and passionate choice-based commitments.

THE SEVEN YEAR ITCH

"There is nothing either good or bad but thinking makes it so."
~ William Shakespeare

It's ironic that I decided to write about the Seven Year Itch as I happen to be at that exact point in my relationship with my husband now. This poses a question which I'm not sure I can answer just yet. Does the Seven Year Itch happen at seven years into a <u>relationship</u>? Or does it only happen seven years into an actual <u>legal marriage</u>? Or do we get to experience it twice? I suppose it's all in the details.

For anyone who may not know what I'm talking about, the Seven Year Itch is a phrase which references the time in a relationship when one or both partners get bored in their relationship and one or the other decides to seek sexual or emotional relations with someone outside the relationship. Many people will say that this most commonly happens at the seven year point and that if someone goes outside the relationship, the person usually then returns happily to their marriage or relationship for the remainder of their time, satisfied to be with only their original partner. For some, it ends the relationship as someone gets caught deceiving their partner and someone gets hurt. The key here is that people recognize this desirous time in a relationship which is commonly considered temporary. Many people maintain their integrity staying completely committed in their relationships but still go through feelings of dissatisfaction and analysis during this time.

Let's look at the psychology of the Seven Year Itch for a moment. There was a movie about this exact subject with Marilyn Monroe which I have not yet actually seen. I'm told it has left a mark on people's minds that the Seven Year Itch cheating will happen to everyone. I will merely protest that I do not necessarily believe in this precise timing of it. I actually think the Seven Year Itch can happen at any time in a relationship and usually does for most people at some point. Keep in mind I'm referring to the "desire" to be with another person outside of your relationship. Not necessarily the actual decision to act on that desire. All human beings experience desires and it's how people respond to them that matters.

To me, the Seven Year Itch is just the equivalent of a person who is feeling a bit underwhelmed in their relationship and it does not automatically mean anything about whether or not a person will cheat. Nor does the Seven Year Itch mean anything about how well a person is keeping their significant other satisfied. I am fairly certain that nearly all people become unsatisfied from time to time during long-term relationships.

People tend to draw circumstances to themselves when they believe something to be true. Therefore, if you are worried about the Seven Year Itch, you may in fact draw circumstances to you that prove the theory. On the other hand, if you are someone who feels like this theory of the Seven Year Itch gives you a "get out of jail free" card, I'd recommend you reconsider. Hurt is hurt and cheating is cheating if you get caught.

I'm going to elaborate on my thoughts about cheating for a moment. I have a saying I always say. "If a guy or girl cheated on his or her partner and never got caught, did it ever happen?" That's my personal rendition of, "If a tree falls in the forest and no one is around to hear it, does it make a sound?" My answer to that question has always been "no." Nothing happened if you don't know that it happened. In your perceived world, you only know what you know. I realize someone reading this is going to be unhappy with me for saying that. Some people, you may be one of them, insist that honesty is the best policy. I, on the other hand, would argue that ignorance is in fact sometimes bliss, when it comes to these types of situations. What you don't know won't hurt you. If it were me, and yes, I've told my husband this; I would NOT want to know if he decided to hook up with someone other than me. Let me live in my fantasy which is truthfully my reality that I'm the only one for him. My rule is simply this... Never put my body at risk by doing something that risks our health.

Consider this for just a minute and then we'll get back to the subject at hand. If your partner truly did something with someone outside your relationship, and in fact regretted it, and you really NEVER knew that it happened, then you would NEVER EVER think about. Therefore, you'd never go through the painful thought process of what you did wrong or what an idiot your partner was to risk everything you had. Isn't remaining in a positive state of mind a better place to be and therefore life to live?

Contemplate this. You attract like energy to yourself. If you are sure that you are the "only one" for your partner, you will attract to yourself the very situation that makes you the "only one" again, even if your partner had a momentary lapse in judgment. To the contrary if you worry about a negative situation, you will inevitably attract to you yet another situation worth worrying about. My personal belief is that the healthiest decision for a person, who made a mistake or choice of this nature, is to keep it to themselves, forgive, and move on. For the record this happens to both men and women. Forgiveness and rehabilitation of oneself is what matters in this case if you are the person doing the cheating.

OK, so back to the point of the Seven Year Itch. The Seven Year Itch can in fact happen at any point in a relationship. It can happen very early on or much later into a relationship. It can certainly happen seven years into a relationship as it is termed and therefore expected, but more than likely because we have been programmed to believe that this is a true phenomenon. I'm not so sure how much more true it is than anything else we choose to believe that is not actually fact. The reality is you will always have attractions in life. This never ends for men or women. It's just a matter of time if you are open at all to connections with other human beings. At some point you will find you are attracted to someone other than just your partner. The question is, what would you do with that attraction if it turned out that you could do anything you wanted to with it? Would you act on it to satisfy your craving? Would you play with the attraction to help fill your ego proving to yourself that you've still got what it takes? Would you walk away disgusted with yourself or the other person, because you insist on doing the right thing? Do you believe you ought to live in the moment and therefore you might as well enjoy it for a minute and then walk away? It's all up to you. I'm not sure there is a right or wrong answer, only the integrity of your word and your intention.

You may have discovered by now I don't always buy into conventional ways of thinking about what is right or wrong and OK or NOT OK, in a relationship. I am a strong believer in personal rights to freedom of choice to believe what you choose to believe. I myself believe people have the right to change their minds and grow and discover and love and learn as they go. Meaning, I don't think anyone on earth has all the answers. I think we all want desperately to have some rules to follow to know we are on the right track, but deep down we all have yearnings and we are all questioning where the fine lines are drawn. If I cross this line or that line, is it really that big of a deal? This may be why many of us go to church to feel as if there are some great rewards for behaving a certain way, or to ask for forgiveness. Life is challenging and we need to be motivated to stay on some track. Yet, at the end of the day, who is really to say? Are we really supposed to be monogamous creatures or is that something someone made up for us because we are so darn jealous by nature that the chaos caused by jealousy outweighs the reward of fulfilling our desires? Therefore, people decided that this particular rule was a keeper or this other one was not.

If you are experiencing fear of the Seven Year Itch for worry that you might lose your partner temporarily to their desires for another person, I'm here to tell you that the greatest gift you can give yourself is the one of self-confidence to shelve it. Forget the fear of the Seven Year Itch. Worrying about your partner cheating is pointless. In other words, get rid of that fear and know that it doesn't really have to happen. On the other hand, it also could happen at any point in a relationship. Why spend any time worrying about it when you can't actually predict what someone is going to do. You have to be secure in yourself and when you are, self-assuredness is the best way of keeping your partner interested in you. You and only you need to know that you are a person who is worth keeping. Self-assuredness is an attractive quality and enough to keep your partner intrigued by you if you exude plenty of it.

If you are a man or a woman who is considering acting on the Seven Year Itch urges, but hoping you can contain your impulses, there are ways to channel this energy such that you don't risk everything you have with your chosen life partner. If you are playing with the idea, remember that everyone gets bored at some point or another. Nobody stays hot to someone forever. It comes and goes throughout any relationship. Studies have shown that during the first year of a relationship humans release elevated levels of chemicals keeping us more highly attracted to our partners. That changes going into year two when those same chemicals are released at much lower levels creating a less euphoric experience. This apparently can happen in any relationship. Nobody is immune. That said, some people are addicted to the chemical releases and will seek partner after partner as soon as they feel as though they are no longer having those experiences of chemically induced euphoria. Others will create drama to start a fight, cause a breakup, and then makeup with the same partner to create the chemical releases again and again. I'm not recommending this. Others still will go into a state of depression about it. Yet these changes that take place throughout the life of a relationship are entirely natural. It happens to all of us. So you might as well accept it at some point and consider channeling this energy into a great cause.

If you've already acted on the Seven Year Itch impulse and you're sure you have not in any way potentially put your loved one's health at risk, let it go, forgive yourself and never tell. That's my advice. What your partner doesn't know will never hurt them. If you are a serial cheater, you may at some point want to analyze what you are getting from this and how you can go deeper spiritually for the satisfaction that you are searching for. I most certainly don't have all the answers here but I can say that nobody is alone when it comes to the experience of dissatisfaction.

Lastly, if you've busted your partner cheating or toying with the idea, please remember that we all have attractions and it does not necessarily mean anything. We are all human and make mistakes. If you can work on forgiving your partner, do it and move on. This will be the best thing in most cases, assuming that you have both decided to work through it. One of the biggest issues with cheating is the probability of it destroying a person's trust. Meaning that you've given your word to someone that they are the only one for you and now you've broken their trust. But let's think about the severity of this. We give and break our word accidentally and often very frequently in life. Who on the planet is perfect? The key is figuring out where on the severity and frequency chart this falls for you? It is different for everyone.

Another issue with cheating is usually that we are so ego driven as human beings that we tend to dwell on comparing ourselves to others, sometimes driving ourselves insane. Remind yourself, even the hottest of movie stars, rock stars and athletes as well as church going religious leaders go through this in relationships. So it's your choice to do what you will with it if you've cheated or been cheated on. Do you choose to dwell on negativity? Or are you with someone who is worth working through these things with?

Life is made up of choices and challenges and we all live with them daily, often thinking we are unique. We are unique in the sense that we are all individuals different from every other person on earth on a molecular and cellular level. However, we are not unique in our experiences in general. In fact we are more than likely simultaneously connected to everyone else on earth as much as we are unique from them. Though no two relationships are alike, we do all feel the human emotions of highs and lows, happiness and depression, sickness and health. We all only go so high and so low and typically survive it. So knowing this, the power is in your hands to do what you will with it, keeping in mind that you are your own person and you don't own nor are you owned by anyone. You choose daily to be with the person you are with and that is enough. The more you are willing to allow your partner to also be themselves, the greater the gift you are to them. That is what creates an attraction. Trust that if you are meant to be together, you will be. If you are together, be fair with your partner by spelling out your expectations so as to set them up for success with you.

We all need to operate with constant forgiveness of ourselves and of others. We all mess up. We all strive to be better. We all feel guilt and remorse (well most of us). We all like adventure and we love to be moved and inspired. We all like to feel special and have a need to be wanted. And we all pride ourselves on doing the right thing when we do it. We are frequently handed opportunities to do things that contribute to our personal growth and awareness and we are often given situations to help us become better people. It's what we do with it that matters. The first step in that process is usually stepping down from our own high horse to remind ourselves that we are all human. The most powerful control you have is over your own perspective. No matter how good or bad you think you have it, there is someone with worse circumstances than you. So take your thinking back to the basics and ask yourself what is really important to you personally. Then decide where to go from there. And always, always practice forgiveness.

INSIGHTS

Understanding Men's Disinterest

1. Typically men are much less interested in marriage than women. This is not always the case, but generally it is.
2. It is not necessarily personal if your man is not anxious to get married or pop the question.
3. There are a ton of reasons why men are disinterested in marriage. Most of which are in their face their entire lives as they witness unhappy marriages everywhere they turn, from their friends, to their own parents and family.
4. Marriage is not easy and clearly does not eliminate problems. Things do change. Women are less likely to admit this ' than men and men tend to thoroughly analyze it prior to proposing, often stalling their actions.

Women's Desire for the Fairy Tale

1. Most ladies deep down have a secret desire to have the fairy tale wedding.
2. If you are a man and with a girl who you know is the one, you should ask the girl to marry you while there is passion and romance in your relationship.
3. Women want to marry while things are passionate.
4. Women's timing with regards to the subject of marriage is frequently different from that of men.
5. Men will have much more leverage in a long term marriage if they proposed prior to a woman's begging for the proposal.
6. Nobody should propose if they are not sure that their partner is on the same page.
7. Marriage should be reserved for mutual choice-based commitments, not for ownership.

The Seven Year Itch

1. The Seven Year Itch may or may not be accurately timed at Seven Years. It can truly happen at any point in a relationship by any person in a relationship if people are open to connections with others.
2. Most people have attractions even after marriage.
3. Some people act on their desires and others refrain from them. What is right or wrong to do still may remain a question, if you believe people should be allowed to connect with others, change their minds, make mistakes and grow.
4. Forgiveness is the greatest gift you can give yourself.
5. There is no right or wrong answer about what to do with an attraction. There is only the integrity you have with your word with another person and yourself.
6. If you are a serial cheater, you may want to work on finding out what it is that is keeping you unsatisfied. Or perhaps you are someone who connects so completely with people that it tends to trigger passions. There may be ways to channel this energy, such that neither you nor others get hurt, when you experience these types of connections.

5

Common Mistakes

NAGGING

*"Nobody wants to be considered a nag. And surely nobody likes a nag.
Some things just nag at me until I become a nag
and that is indeed annoying."*
~ Julieanne-ism

Nobody reading this book ever nags, right? When I hear my own nagging it really does annoy even me. After all, if I'm nagging, in my mind, I'm simply trying to help make a needed correction for an aggravating mistake or habit. Usually one that is recurring. I mean really as women we feel like what we say just never sinks in at times causing the exasperating nag that slips out of us. As for men, I'm sure they too have their reasons.

Let's discuss the "there's a daddy way" theory. A neighbor once gave me a wonderful piece of advice. She said to remember as you become a new mother that "there's a daddy way." In other words, your way is not the only way. Fathers also deserve to be able to do things without your constant bossing or instruction. This can go for both men and women and certainly applies whether or not you have children and whether or not you're married. The point is simple. We all need to relax and remember there are at least two personalities in any relationship. That means that there are two distinctly different people who have been raised by different parents and with different circumstances who are supposed to be operating together as a single unit. This means both people in a relationship have to give and take and usually neither wants to be nagged. Letting go of your need to have things a certain way can greatly improve your life. On the other hand, if you trigger annoyances in your spouse or partner who has specific pet peeves, it is great if you can make an effort to change whatever it is that you are doing that annoys them. There are more important things to spend your energy on such as playful things, philosophy, religion and saving the planet.

All in all, this sounds fairly simple but might not always be. Next time you get the urge to complain about something which has been annoying you, stop yourself and just do something about it with a nice energy. Keep in mind this may still trigger something in the other person as they are likely already used to you being annoyed by whatever it is. So the first few times you try to fix things, your partner may not even believe that you are doing something about it with kind energy. They may think you're mad. Allow them time to work through this trigger that has been created until they come around to realizing that you've decided to stop nagging and you've accepted this thing that they do that bugs you. You've now decided you are simply going to sweetly do something about this thing when you want it to be altered as you've made up your mind you don't need them to change to make you happy. You are practicing acceptance.

My husband annoyed me for years with his messy use of our

kitchen. "Can you pleeeeease help out just a bit to minimize my stress by pushing everything on the counter to one side so as to reduce the feeling of everything being spread out all over the place?!" I would nag in a condescending voice. He could not remember to do it. Nor could he remember to put trash in a trash can rather than in the sink or dishes with food on them into the side of the sink with a garbage disposal. So many pet peeves. So I'd bitch about one thing or another inevitably every time he used the kitchen it seemed.

One day I realized I was not making an impact on my husband with getting him to change the way he cleaned up after himself in the kitchen and instead I had become a complete nag. I decided I needed to change myself and stop trying to change him. So one day I began cleaning the kitchen after he made a mess and I was seriously annoyed as I slammed the dishes into the dishwasher. Again another day. Each time, becoming more accustomed to cleaning up after him and each time becoming less and less abrupt about it. In the interim I created a trigger in my husband. My husband knew I was annoyed when I'd go to clean at first. So quickly he became angry by my cleaning. I was over the irritation soon enough but every time I'd touch a dish, he'd run in and shout with near rage in his voice "I was just about to clean up!"

Eventually, and it took a while, I was able to help him remove his trigger by constantly reassuring him that I was not mad when I went to clean the kitchen. I was long past being mad about it. I had to literally remind him that we shared the house and that it was OK for me to clean as well as him and that again I was not mad while doing it. Finally, now, he allows me in the kitchen to clean without feeling uptight and I do it without frustration. What's more, is that he has begun to clean up immediately after cooking leaving me very few instances where I have to jump in and clean. And he does it with a smile. We have completely restored harmony to our kitchen.

Lastly, a reminder to the men, it is not just women who nag! Men, you can be the best of naggers at times. So whoever it is doing it, take responsibility and change it. Put that energy you spend nagging into simply changing the thing that bothers you. Put away the laundry, wipe down the counter, clean out the car or put the toilet seat down. Fix whatever it is that is bugging you rather than bitch about it. Your energy will be better spent changing it than attempting to change someone else's habits that bother you. This will be much healthier for your relationship. And who knows, you may even find the other person begins contributing to the very thing that needs changing.

LADIES, STOP APOLOGIZING

"When a girl really lets me have it for something I've done wrong, I have tons of respect for her. But almost always, she turns around and apologizes, essentially taking it back. I like a woman who stands her ground and who isn't afraid to say what's acceptable or not. That's hot!"
~ *Mark O'Connor*

Nine out of ten men will tell you that an attractive woman has an opinion and when put to the test she is confident enough to say what she really thinks. She is not someone who then turns around and apologizes over and over in an attempt to hang on to her man. In fact, even if she is harsh in speaking her mind regarding boundaries that have been crossed by a guy, she should still stand her ground. There is the case when a woman says something that is mean spirited which probably qualifies for an apology. Let's be clear as to the difference. If a man has, for example, cheated on you (assuming you're the woman in this case) and you say, "I deserve better and you had better straighten up or you're going to lose me once and for all!" It should be left at that. Simple personal boundaries. You are a strong woman who deserves to be treated with respect and you've stated it. The woman who continues on soon after making a strong statement about her boundaries with, "I'm so sorry and I love you so much and would do anything for you..."

has taken away her own power, diminished her sex appeal and given permission to her man to go out and repeat the mistake again.

If on the other hand your man forgot to put his dish in the dishwasher and you cursed his name for it, this may actually merit an apology. Certainly when we say things from a hormonal place, we often owe men apologies. It's OK in those cases to apologize for your tone and emotion. However, again, when you've told a guy about a serious boundary that's been crossed and you've stated it from a strong place (perhaps even anger), you do NOT need to turn around and apologize. I have guy friends, both hot and not, who will tell you that this is true for them. When a girl puts them in their place they actually find it quite attractive. However, the second the lady takes it back out of fear for pushing him away, he too is taken back and finds it both confusing and unfortunately unattractive.

The message is simple. If you are a man or a woman, but especially if you are a woman, who has personal boundaries that have been crossed by your significant other, whatever they may be, state your truth and stand your ground! NO MORE apologies! We are all guilty of this. Women tend to nurture and want to please and therefore feel guilty when they act out of a place of strength. Women are strong creatures and that very strength is extremely attractive to others. By operating with strength it can help you to surround yourself with people who treat you with respect. Without being cruel, it's OK to say what's on your mind and certainly OK to put your foot down on what is right for you! Let everything else naturally find its place around that core. Above all else, stop apologizing for it!

INSIGHTS

<u>Nagging</u>

1. Nobody wants to be nagged.
2. Nobody wants to be considered a nag.
3. Everybody has their own way.
4. Rather than nag, put that energy towards doing whatever it is that needs to be done.

<u>Ladies, Stop Apologizing</u>

1. Men find women who have and express an opinion extremely attractive.
2. Apologies take away power, diminish sex appeal and give permission to others to repeat what they've done that upset you to begin with.
3. The only appropriate apology is if you delivered an inappropriate message fueled by callus anger.
4. If you have personal boundaries that are crossed by another person, whatever they may be, state your truth and stand your ground! NO MORE apologies!

6

Insights On and For Men

PORN

"I don't watch porn with dialogue. I'm far beyond that."
~ Seth Rogen

"They act in porn?"
~ Anonymous Man

A really good guy I know once told me "You're NOT a 'real' guy if you don't have Porn on your computer! – You should put that in your book!"

Here it is! Spelling it out, in my book, a section about porn. A short section but a section none-the-less. Ladies, here's the bottom line. If you find Porn on your man's computer, you are NOT alone. In fact, you are not even in the minority. My most sincere advice is this: Do NOT go looking for it! In addition, it means absolutely nothing about your relationship. It really says nothing about how happy your man is with you or how good or bad your sex life is. In fact, in many cases it may be helping your sex life. I'm not a man but what I do know is that lots of men have a thing about porn. Let's face it, they are visually stimulated creatures. Do not take it personally.

Now Men! A word of advice to you, keep it private! Clean up your computer. It's really easy to accidentally stumble upon snippets of pictures from the porn sites you've visited because whether you realize it or not computers save these random images in often unknown places.

One of the handfuls of times I stumbled across pictures of hot naked women on my husband's computer was when I simply went to save a file that was emailed to me and happened to need to borrow his computer to do it that day. It opened up a temporary folder automatically that had saved some of the pictures of random hot women he'd looked at. So I actually did NOT go looking for it. I found it by accident. Unfortunately it was of a bunch of women that looked NOTHING LIKE ME! So I took it personally for a moment. They were blonds with large breasts. I am a brunette with small breasts. These innocent looking girls were getting naked in the woods. And so it is. I think I would have been flattered at least if some of them had been my type. But nope! Not one. If you're a guy looking at porn, at least look at a couple girls of your lady's type in the event that she should ever stumble across the pictures on your computer. Oh and who knows, maybe that might even remind you of your lady! I have to just say this once. What sweet, hot lady with any brains allows people to take pictures of her with her pants around her ankles? Come on, how is that hot?! OK, whatever. I concede, it was pretty hot but that's not the point!

Ladies, let me reiterate, unless you are looking for a reason to spice up your relationship with a little guilt trip or a good fight, don't go looking for porn on your man's computer!

Men, hide it better! Clean up your computer. Or stay off the sites. Once we come across it we cannot help but to compare ourselves to the women you were looking at and yes, we are going to hold it against you. Our egos are still our egos and we have a very difficult time forgetting these injustices to our supposedly sacred hearts! Just ask yourself, what if your woman saved to her computer a bunch of videos of sexy confident men in uniform, committing random acts of romance and professing their undying love while simultaneously practicing great listening skills. I mean how would you compete with that?!

LOVE AND ORGASMS - WHAT'S REAL?

"The period after orgasm (known as a refractory period) is often a relaxing experience, attributed to the release of the neurohormones oxytocin and prolactin, as well as endorphins (or 'endogenous morphine')."
~ *Wikipedia*

"Morphine has high potential for addiction; tolerance and psychological dependence develop rapidly, although physiological dependence may take several months to develop."
~ *Wikipedia*

Regarding LOVE and Orgasms, what's truly real? Sometimes, you just need to get laid or have a good orgasm! Who cares if in your imagination a fantasy person does the job for you? Oh wait though. Caution: If your fantasy person is someone you know personally, you may become unreasonably attracted or addicted to them.

Human beings are addicted to danger, love, passion and romance. Addicted to adrenalin. Addicted to chemical releases. Let's take an office place romance as an example or any affair. Why would a guy risk everything he had with a happy wife and kids to have a fling with his secretary? What made a powerful president risk everything with an intern? Is it just another opportunity to get laid? Or could it also have something to do with the attraction to danger?

Let's look at a woman's reason for an affair. Women love

romance. Women also love men who are powerful and hard to get. In office place settings men love danger but are afraid of being accused of sexual harassment so they approach women with restraint which women find attractive. Men also find women who practice restraint much more attractive. Naturally when all parties have a reason to be discreet or practice restraint it causes extraordinary tension. Abnormal intensity is nearly always found in forbidden love or romance. It's often the type of intensity that would not exist if it were not in fact forbidden.

Did you know that you can actually fall in love with a person after having an orgasm? In fact even if you were only thinking about the person when you got off, you could potentially fall in love with them. Seem too crazy to be true? An orgasm stimulates certain hormones in your brain causing you to feel euphoric, triggering the part of the brain that forges bonding and attachment. Therefore, you could potentially sleep with or even simply fantasize about your worst enemy and unexpectedly fall in love with or become infatuated by them. Ever have a dream about someone random and wake up the next day and suddenly and sometimes forever more you find yourself attracted to them?

When it comes to the chemical releases in our bodies caused by sex, love, intense attractions, and danger we can literally experience feelings similar to those feelings felt by people using stimulants such as morphine or cocaine. Your brain can actually believe something to be true that may in fact not be real. You may believe someone to be the greatest thing since sliced bread, then you later find yourself saying, "Self, what the hell were you thinking?" No need to be hard on yourself, you just suffered a temporary acid trip. One that can be as equally exhilarating as it can be excruciating. The reality is that when this happens in a prohibited situation, many people lack self-control. Often, serious self-control is necessary to practice the level of discretion needed to prevent actions that can lead to forbidden pleasure, fixation and often obsession.

94

When people newly fall into a state of intense love or infatuation, they commonly become immersed in their newfound passionate feelings. Initially, they are unable to focus and become distracted by a constant state of awareness of the feelings that are overwhelming them. Everyone around them can see it on their face, in their energy and in everything they do. They become abnormally energized and motivated and sometimes equally devastated and desperate depending on the level of reciprocation by the person they fall for. Keep in mind, some of this can happen in a moment and nothing was ever acted upon. If not acted upon, the feelings often subside more quickly. Though not always.

If you're one of the lucky ones who found the great love of your life and you have been with them for a period of time without dramatic ups and downs of constant fights and bouts of jealousy, then you know that the chemically induced state referenced above eventually wears off and you have to then face the person head on without the drug-like euphoric state that you once experienced. You have to learn to endure the next part of your life with the sometimes harsh realities of who this very normal "not so God-like" person might actually be. This is when you learn whether or not you're the type of person who can settle into a more calm state of being with fewer highs and lows. You might have to become the type of person who accepts life with this person without the adrenalin rush you originally enjoyed. Maybe you were once a monk and understand the type of contentment that I'm referencing. If you're like the rest of us, you say to yourself, "Shit, this is it?" And then you endure the realities of annoying habits, the difficult task of committed loyalty and the usual waves of crazy thoughts and guilt along the way. If this is your new phase of exploration at the current time and if you're a man please refer to the section on "porn." If you're a woman and your man has resorted to porn and you know about it, please refer to the section on "porn." If you're a woman and you do not yet know about your man's obsession with porn, please refer to the

95

section on "porn." Lastly, if you have not yet read the section on "porn" please refer to the section on "porn."

OK, all kidding aside, truly, the tendency with humans is that we begin to seek new stimulants to create states of euphoria once previously experienced during the first year of passion. Similar outlets may include alcohol, drugs, forbidden sex and torrid affairs, jumping from a plane or cliff diving. Yet suddenly unlike during that first year when you were willing to literally and seriously DIE for your new love at the drop of a hat, you begin to contemplate whether or not you would actually still take that bullet for them after all, or possibly prefer to become the shooter. You suddenly ensure your spouse has a solid life insurance policy and you notice they do the same. Or you count your blessings and begin to imagine what you want when you are in your rocking chair sitting on your front porch someday. Oh and many still experiment with or begin using some addictive stimulant to fill that void of no longer feeling the euphoria of new love.

If you already have children you might begin considering the legacy you'd like to leave behind. Or perhaps you would merely like to choose more healthy and less risky outlets to change up the monotony of your day to day existence. Examples might include going to church, taking vacations together, having dinner parties with friends, working out together or taking classes together. But let's admit it. How much fun is that compared to cliff diving or taboo affairs? Well vacations yes. But church? Really?! In all seriousness, religious or spiritual conquests especially when shared by like faith partners can be incredibly bonding and can help people grow together. No two people think completely alike on the subject of religion, let alone anything else, but spiritual outlets can often help with bonding. Why not also consider ongoing hot sex with your chosen partner so that you can reunite that link created by a good orgasm. Regardless of how much you still want to look at the other person, you can still have hot sex with them, if you just use your imagination.

Everything is always either getting better or getting worse in a love relationship. Nothing is ever simply stagnant. That is not to say that your commitment to love with a person changes, just that the effectiveness of your communication and how you bond will go through changes. If your relationship seems stagnant it is likely getting worse. Actively and consciously working on relationship skills can actually be a lot of fun and can inspire others. Many people like to keep their "story" private, playing the part of perfect societal couples. That in fact, is not inspiring. Everyone has some desire to be able to relate. I'm here to say that no matter who you are, you are not alone. Ups and downs happen. Too bad more people don't admit it when it comes to their relationships so we could all feel a little less frustrated by our seemingly unique situations.

For those of you in the blissful period... Enjoy it! When it changes, remember you are not alone and there are numerous healthy things you can do to spice up any relationship. Keep relating, spell out expectations, and actively make it a point to have healthy communication.

AN ENCOUNTER WITH AN EX - LIE VS. FULL DISCLOSURE

"Integrity is telling a lie and sticking to it."
~ Anonymous

"To be trusted is a greater compliment than being loved."
~ George MacDonald

This section is primarily for the men, however, ladies, please note: If you are in a situation where your man has just made you jealous with an encounter with an ex or any other woman, or he has done something that you absolutely cannot tolerate, your only job is to spell it out for him. Give him a shot at fixing it if he's someone you're committed to working things out with, and remember men deserve your perspective delivered clearly as they cannot read accurately between the lines. Hopefully, your man will get to this book before you meet. In the case where your partner has already triggered your jealousy, the solution is simply to spell it out for them. Take that mind chatter you have going on in your brain and put it on paper. Leave out all the hurtful comments and your grasping jealous needs to insult your man or another woman and simply spell out what you want or need. I will also do that for the men so it's crystal clear what we need as women.

OK, a man in a committed relationship has just encountered, yep "accidentally" stumbled across one of his exes, from his not-so-distant or possibly distant past. On occasion ladies, the "accidental" part may be true. Other times, perhaps, your man has been secretly hoping for this day. Let's always default to trusting their under explained story that leaves you wanting still more information, often the details of which are too convoluted to decipher anyway. For the record men, women will almost always want a lot of details when it comes to hearing about your encounter with an ex.

There are two possible scenarios when a man runs into one of his exes. One is that the ex-girlfriend is clearly not desired. Let's assume that this is not going to create jealousy. When she is truly undesired by a man, he will offer FULL DISCLOSURE. Telling you details with ease and more than likely completely true. This is not something which requires any energy whatsoever. You will know the difference. Nobody in this situation should create unnecessary drama around an ex.

Scenario two is that this ex-girlfriend is someone that this man has secretly missed, been curious about or got dumped by, therefore always leaving a taste of desire in his mouth. Or a girl who told him "no," thereby not technically an ex but no less desirous or hurtful! The bottom line ladies, is that these girls exist and there is nothing any of us can do about it. They exist.

Occasionally as a woman you may not care if your man stumbles across an ex. In fact you may be one of the girls who you yourself secretly misses your own ex. In this case your

98

current man may even be doting on you now (and it may even be smothering you – you know who you are) while you are thinking about this other guy that you miss. Clearly this can happen with either gender. More often however, it's a woman who gets bent out of shape by her man's encounter with an ex.

Let me spell this out for the men if you've just encountered an ex and you are overly excited about it.

#1: Decide quickly and commit if you are going to disclose this information. You've run into your ex! If you are going to lie to your current partner about your encounter, here's my very simple and only advice. Be smart, lie completely! NEVER get caught. That's right! If you lie so thoroughly without ever creating suspicion and we truly never know, everything is gravy. You will not be questioned because your lady will continue believing she is the most important woman in the world to you. Note of caution: You've heard the saying, "You are only as sick as the secrets you keep." So let it go once you've done the deed. Only you will have to stomach this decision to keep this information a lie. Women are simple. We just don't want our hearts broken and if you lie and get caught, we will make you pay! One way or another! I realize this may seem extreme considering we are not saying you cheated with your ex here. I'm only suggesting that you've run across your ex. Nonetheless if you lie now and slip up and mention it a month later, we will seriously question why you didn't fully disclose it to begin with.

Men, you will NOT have an opportunity to be wishy-washy about how much you want to tell the truth. Any decision you make to lie, about an encounter with an ex, had better be made fully and fast or your partner will sniff out your lie so fast, you will believe in women's intuition if you didn't already. A woman has the ability to make a man's life miserable if she is questioning his integrity. Meanwhile, men tend to be quite defensive when explaining a half-truth. This can both frustrate the man and hurt the woman. So lie completely or don't lie at all.

#2: Regarding FULL DISCLOSURE. Let me define this for you if you are a man because I can assure you that prior to this book you've never truly understood what this meant. Full disclosure means the complete truth. It means telling your lady the details and I do mean in detail. If we ask, give it to us. You might as well let us get fully upset once and for all which also validates our feelings helping us to more quickly resolve the situation. So give it to us straight and then move forward.

If you're a woman, forgive your man if you believe he still has feelings for an ex that he has simply run across. As long as he gets past it and is with you, you can let it go and be confident that you are the one. We don't own people and we all have feelings for others. This is natural and common. So just be in the moment and let the past go. Your man's issues with resolving old feelings, if he has them, are his issue, not yours. So let him work through them on his own as you would expect if you were going through the same. Also, remember there is no harm in a man running across his ex. Sleeping with her while he's with you, yes, perhaps, but simply stumbling upon her in passing means nothing whether or not your man still has feelings for her.

OK, a quick personal story on this. My husband was in love with a girl who broke his heart before he met me. Probably many actually. But while we were together it was obvious he had some feelings for one particular girl for a period of time. I was crazy about my husband in our dating days so you can imagine this was a painful experience for me. He stumbled across his ex, one day on the internet early in our relationship. This turned in to his coming up with a reason to try and see her in another state at the time. It was a legitimate reason on paper, but very much not OK in my mind, with my intense jealousy of her at the time. When I would bring it up or press him about her, it made him extremely agro. He did not offer the type of support I most needed when this was happening and I could feel him pull away as I expressed my jealousy. I didn't want to lose him so I mustered up the confidence to know that I was the prize and to give him the space he needed to see it. I had witnessed enough suffering in other people's poor decisions in relationships to know I needed to stop the vicious cycle of jealousy and defensiveness that had been created. I'm here to tell you it was not easy at the time. He truly hadn't done anything wrong. He simply had feelings still for someone that he had at one time been in love with. I only realized it because of his defensiveness about her when I'd bring her up.

What my husband could have done differently at the time to help me through my jealousy, might have been to simply acknowledge my feelings and give me extra reassurance. I still would have had to overcome my jealousy. We were in a new relationship at the time and one or the other of us had to make the effort to work through it with maturity if we were going to stay strong as a couple. At the time it had to be me. You can't after all fault someone for having feelings for someone they once loved. He and I both laugh about it now and he no longer has the feelings for her that he once had. But at the time, I assure you it was not easy for either of us.

If you know you're going down a slippery slope with your lack of willpower or jealousy, remember you cannot change other people. Do whatever you can to get a grip. Look in the mirror and remind yourself that you're the prize. Then step back, give space and watch the magic happen.

If you are the person causing jealousy, be sure to offer your partner reassurance. This can go a long way regardless of where your loyalties lie. At the end of the day, the bottom line is simple. When it comes to a lie vs. full disclosure, consider who is involved, reflect on your actions, think about the consequences and remember to be decisive. Only you will know what to do.

LISTENING - WHAT? HUH?

"Home is where you can say anything you like 'cause nobody listens to you anyway."
~ Unknown

"My wife says I never listen to her. At least I think that's what she said."
~ Unknown

"Did you hear what I said? I said did you hear what I said?!" These two sentences may rank up there as two of the most overused statements in my house. I am still trying to work through this particular aspect of men. Truly, I do not know what it would take at times to get my husband to really listen to me. His favorite thing to do when I completely bust him not listening, is to focus for a second and then repeat the last line of whatever it was that I said as if to try and prove to me that he was listening. I'm still trying to impress upon him that it's not about "proving" that he just absorbed something I said in his subconscious mind enough to regurgitate it to me. It's about me needing to actually feel like I'm being listened to. In fact, I must admit, I'd rather feel like I'm being heard than to actually be heard at times.

Let's face it, women need to talk. With girlfriends, sisters, mothers, daughters and dogs we are often heard better than we are by our male partners. I can see why men like to get together with other men because none of them have to listen to drawn out details about someone's day or issues and they can all sit in silence watching a game or playing a video game or doing whatever guys do. Guys do in fact have conversation I've noticed but rarely is it anything like that of their conversations with women. No wonder they never stop for directions. I mean why stop for directions if you are not going to listen to them anyway! I'm kidding. OK, more on that later when we discuss why not to tell men what to do or how to do it, a section that the men will appreciate.

Men don't seem to have a need for the detailed <u>back and forth</u> communication the way that women do. When a woman speaks she really wants it to land on the other person, eliciting a response that lets her know it did indeed land. Then she likes to continue on in the same fashion for a while again and again with responses that communicate to her that she is being understood. She's not asking for advice or a solution necessarily. She simply wants to know someone cares enough to listen to what she is talking about.

When a woman interacts with a man, with her daily discussions about life, it is probably a rare occasion when a man sincerely cares. This is not to say he does not care about the woman. Men have a tendency to prefer concise to the point conversation without the details and without all the "story." In fact if men had it their way, they'd really like to hear the punch line or the point of the story first. Then they'd be more likely to let the ladies fill in the details. If you're a man, FAKE IT already! Allow your woman to set the stage with a tremendous amount of unnecessary build up. I realize it probably takes a considerable effort since it is contrary to your nature but pretend to care long enough for her to empty what's on her mind. For women this is an absolutely necessary form of therapy.

If you're a guy and you want to keep your lady happy, there's no greater gift you can give her than to really hear her out when she needs to talk. How hard can it be? OK, granted, maybe it is hard. Suck it up on occasion though so your woman can have a little reprieve. She needs it. It's a must for her to survive in this tough world. And trust me when I say that if you listen the first time around it will save you from listening to a whole lot more later on, when the fury is unleashed for your not having heard her the first time. By prolonging the inevitable you cause the very abuse you receive later on. You know that unnecessary mishandling you feel like you get that seems to come from nowhere. That actually stems from your woman not having been able to download what was originally on her mind when she needed to. It simply escalated to the place where she snapped about something quite different. By the time we ladies blow, it usually has nothing to do with the original nagging cause of our distress which would have gone away had we just been able to speak freely about it and feel like we were heard.

You can imagine what my husband has to contend with being married to an author who is studying and writing about the differences between men and women. Of course he is aware of my practice of my own tips on him. I still have a tendency at times to hope in a futile attempt that he will pick up on the hints I give him. There are just some days I feel like I should NOT have to spell it out for him. I'm wrong. For example, moments ago I was attempting to tell him something and he stood up and walked away while I was talking to him. This is a common unconscious occurrence on his part. I frequently find myself talking louder as he gets further away as if that will get my message across. Ha. He already tuned me out. Let's be honest, he probably never tuned in.

I'm quite sure the sound of my voice is similar to that of subtle relaxing background music to him. More common even, with my husband is that he begins doing Yoga or other types of meditative exercises while I'm speaking to him. I actually continue talking and now throw in remarks for my own amusement, such as, "Honey, I really think it's especially healthy for you to have a good chat while doing your peaceful yoga practice." Or I will just throw in a random absurd comment such as "...and then the purple cow jumped over the moon and down came a large caterpillar with a huge penis..." That's my idea of self-soothing entertainment as it is obviously ridiculous. Of course he doesn't laugh as he clearly didn't hear me. Nor does he speak or respond or even look at me for that matter. You can imagine how much I feel like I'm being paid attention to. Today, I decided to drop what I thought would be a gigantic hint that was of course NOT received. I said, "I really think that it is worth the money to pay a therapist to listen to me." I continued, "I believe one hour a week of undivided attention from someone-anyone who really listened to me would suffice."

He replied with, "uh huh."

Needless to say, he did not get the hint. That or maybe he was hoping I would hire a therapist for listening, to free him up from the heavy lifting. I even took it a step further and read what I just wrote to my husband out loud in an attempt that he should really take it in.

He replied with, "Honey, that's a great section."

Again, another example of how hints don't hit. I was hoping he would say, "Sweetheart, what was it you were trying to tell me?" Still no awareness of his inability to listen to, or take in what I wanted to communicate. The moral of this story is simple. You really have to spell it out for your man if you need his undivided attention.

If you're a woman here's what you can do to make your life a little easier when trying to communicate with the opposite sex. First and foremost, do NOT and I repeat, do NOT download on a man when he is first returning home after a long day at work. This is very bad timing. He needs to spend some time unwinding and doing whatever it is that he needs to do before he will be ready to listen. You will also find that you have much more success if you ask a man if he has a little time to listen.

I realize scheduling time with your own partner to be heard seems a bit much, but if you really need to be heard, this is how you may need to approach a man. "Excuse me dear. I know you've been very busy. I love you. I am so proud of you and grateful for how hard you work and for how well you take care of me. I was wondering if you might have a little bit of time to listen to something I want to talk to you about. Also, I realize this may not even be that important to you, but what I really need is to speak to someone who is willing to listen. Would you be willing to listen for a little bit and just let me know you understand how I'm feeling?" OK, let's face it that was too much. He tuned out at "Excuse me dear."

Let's try a different approach. "Honey, I need to download some stupid shit that doesn't matter. Having someone to listen to me would be the equivalent of oxygen right now. You think you could give me a little time and pretend like you care? I'll make it up to you with a good blow job." And watch the reception you get. Mind you, he may not have heard the first couple sentences but he will have definitely tuned in to that last sentence. And he'll rewind in his subconscious to hear the prior sentence or two and he'll make the time I promise. This type of explanation for your man is truly what *Spelling It Out for Your Man* is all about. It can work wonders in your communication.

If you are a man and you really are <u>not</u> in the mood to hear out a woman, please respond with something like, "Honey, love of my life, I fully hear you and know you need me to listen to you. I love you so much. I'm extremely tired right now and really want to hear you out. Would it be OK with you if we do this in another 15 minutes after I get a beer and take a quick shower so I can give you the undivided attention you deserve?" And watch how your lady turns to putty. She may even give you that blow job before the talk. You just never know.

Lastly, for the men, women need to be heard but do not necessarily need your advice. Your opinion if it matches hers is A-OK. If it doesn't sync and a woman is venting, it might be best to keep your opinion to yourself. Just let your woman vent. She needs to download without you fixing anything for her. It's OK to let a woman know that you're still listening by saying things like, "Oh, uh huh, really? Wow, you're kidding." Keep in mind, right when you think she's done, give it more time. She's probably not finished. If you let her empty completely it will save you from another outburst. Men, this may take three times as long as it would take you. So keep on keeping on! You'll get there, to the end, eventually and be released from these painful duties. Then your woman will quickly forgive and forget all wrongdoings that led her to this point.

Ladies, as a reminder, unlike how we love the build-up, men

want to get to the point. Men love the end of the story first. If you want a man to listen while you fill in all the details tell him the point first and then your guy can relax as you elaborate. Listening may not seem to be a man's forte, but remember, we all have different ways of communicating. The key is to be conscious of your partner's ways. The more we all become mindful of each other, the easier communication will become.

LET A MAN BE A MAN, WHY NOT TO TELL A MAN WHAT TO DO

"The trouble with advice is that it's usually something
you don't want to hear."
~ *Charles De Lint*

In the beginning when you first fall in love with a man, he can do no wrong. He sweeps you off your feet. He rides in as your knight in shining armor and becomes your protector. He fixes things for you and you love it. He makes you feel safe. He frequently saves the day, helping you with any need that you have. You can ask him for anything and he'll find a way to make it happen. You're in love and he can do no wrong. He can drive like a maniac and if you died on this day, it would be OK, so long as you were together. You are infatuated. You trust him. You love him. Nothing matters more than pleasing him and you do everything in your power to make sure he is satisfied with only you. You make him feel like a man.

Then something happens. You move-in together or get married. Oh, ugh. Suddenly, you realize he doesn't put the toilet seat down, he leaves dirty dishes in the sink, he rarely wipes up after himself and can't he see that if he just did some things a certain way, it would make his life so much easier. And wow, doesn't he realize that switching lanes all the time doesn't really speed up the commute? God forbid he finds a parking space without your suggestions. Who knows how he got through a single day alone before you came along. And you begin telling him, little by little, sweetly at first. "Honey, you forgot the cap on the toothpaste. No worries, I got it." "Babe, if you turn in here you'll find a better parking spot." "Sweetheart, that burner is a little hot you might want to turn it down." "Babe, slow down." "Whoa, what are you doing?" "You left the cap off the toothpaste again." "You forgot to put the milk away." "Would you PLEEEEASE put the toilet seat down?!" "Watch out!" "Look out!" "Would you just shut the door?!" "What the Fuck?!" "You make me crazy!"

Suddenly your man goes from being on top of the world, powerful, strong and invincible, to behaving like that of a small child who frequently messes up everything. He slowly but surely starts to hesitate when he goes to fix things in an attempt to make sure he does it the way you'd want him to. In so doing, he screws it up more. He stops producing the elevated amounts of testosterone he once did as his manhood is slowly but surely being squashed moment by moment. He soon feels compelled to go off and work on a car, play a video game, hang out with the guys and maybe in extreme cases run off with another woman who makes him feel like a man again. Get the point?

Ask yourself, what's the worst case scenario if you really let your man do things his way? Maybe sometimes he'd choose a harder path. Maybe he'd sometimes screw it up. Ultimately he would maintain his manhood, thereby reinforcing his instincts which do in fact protect your family in the end. When a man is allowed to be a man, he will be a better partner and he will appreciate you for it. The next time you get the urge to tell your man what to do, stop for a second and make the decision to simply let it slide. Let your knight in shining armor save the day without your help.

INSIGHTS

Porn

1. Porn happens.
2. Finding Porn on your man's computer is not a surprise, nor does it put you into a category of unique.
3. If your man looks at porn it does NOT necessarily mean anything about your relationship.
4. Men are visually stimulated creatures.
5. Men should take measures to clean up their computers. Keep porn private.
6. Women, don't go looking for it. Give your man a touch of privacy.

Love and Orgasms - What's Real?

1. An orgasm stimulates certain hormones in your brain causing you to feel a type of euphoria that then triggers the part of the brain that forges bonding and attachment.
2. You could potentially fall in love with someone you don't even like because you fantasized about them while having an orgasm.
3. Once the euphoria caused by chemical releases in the body wears off, most people find themselves trying to replace the highs.
4. There are healthy outlets for continued bonding after the chemical releases caused by new love and orgasms become less intense.
5. Things are always getting better or getting worse in a relationship. Nothing is ever stagnant.
6. Actively seeking positive ways to improve your bonding with your partner can be inspiring.

An Encounter with an Ex - Lie vs. Full Disclosure

1. Men and women both have ex-boyfriends, ex-girlfriends, ex-lovers, exes in general. Almost everyone has to accept this.
2. An encounter with an ex at some point in your relationship is possible, even likely.
3. There are two choices when you encounter an ex while in a committed relationship. 1) Tell your new partner or 2) keep it confidential.
4. If you encounter an ex and there is nothing to hide, full disclosure is the logical choice.
5. If you encounter an ex who you are still secretly in love with, you need to make up your mind quickly about your personal policy on disclosure. If you are going to lie or keep it confidential, you should commit fully and do your best to never get caught in your lie.
6. If you are going to offer partial disclosure, it will likely become a problem.
7. Women, men do not read between the lines well. If you need to set the record straight or draw boundaries on this subject, you need to be crystal clear as to your expectations.
8. Women, forgive your man if you believe he still has feelings for an ex. As long as he gets past it and is with you, you can let it go and be confident that you are the one.

Listening - What? Huh?

1. It's not that men don't listen; it's that they can only concentrate on one thing at a time. And usually it is not on what you are saying.
2. If your man doesn't listen, you're not alone.
3. In most cases men have to drop everything to really listen to a woman the way she expects to be listened to.

4. If you need to be heard, it can be useful to explain to your man that you need his undivided attention so he stops and gives you what you need.
5. Don't expect a man to know you need his undivided attention. Consider spelling it out for him.
6. Women really need to be heard out.
7. If you are a guy and you don't hear your woman out, she may eventually end up personally attacking you on an unrelated issue. Hear her out to avoid unnecessary escalation.
8. Never download on a man when he first arrives home after a hard day's work.
9. If you're feeling the build-up of a desperate need to be heard, schedule time with your man to have him listen to you.
10. What's important to a woman may not be important to a man.
11. It's OK to acknowledge that you need to download some stupid shit to your partner.
12. Men, act like your lady's seemingly over detailed description of stupid information is urgently important. Nod and say, "Oh, uh huh, really? Wow, you're kidding."
13. Ladies just need to vent. They don't need a man's advice.
14. Men love the end of the story first. Tell them the point, and then fill in the details after.

Let a Man be a Man - Why Not to Tell a Man What to Do

1. Men can do no wrong when women are first in love with them and then they get comfortable.
2. Eventually when women get comfortable in a relationship they often begin to criticize their partners.
3. When they are frequently being told what to do men begin to lose their instincts in an attempt to please their women.

4. Eventually men will need to seek those things which increase their testosterone levels from other sources if they no longer feel like a man in their own home.

5. Men need to be allowed to make mistakes without being criticized for them.

6. The next time you get the urge to correct a man, stop and allow him to figure things out on his own. It will serve everyone concerned in the long run.

7

I Got Needs and They're Multiplying

ALONE TIME

"Finding some quiet time in your life, I think, is hugely important."
~ Mariel Hemingway

"Your core being is like that of a calm pond. When left alone, your ability to reflect becomes clear."
~ Julieanne-ism

Everyone in a relationship needs alone time now and again. Some people more than others. And some who think they prefer not to have the alone time, probably need it the most. For some, finding alone time is easy. For others, finding alone time seems nearly impossible depending on whether or not you have kids, jobs, pets and/or a checklist a mile long of things to get done. Finding alone time in a relationship is as essential as

113

air and water for a healthy life. Men especially need to go into their "caves" as most of us are now aware. That place where they can just "be" or be left alone. For some women, alone time may actually end up being "away" time rather than "alone" time. Meaning they go out and spend some time with other women, go shopping or take a class. The bottom line is everyone should take their alone time.

The usual problem with alone time is not typically in having our own alone time but rather in allowing our partner or loved one to have theirs. Yet the common human need to hold on to someone is the very thing that can often push a person away. It does more for attraction to allow a man to have his space than it does to be with him every moment. When a woman freely allows a man to go to his cave and just be left alone for a period of time, it will give him the much needed male nourishment that he desperately requires.

For some men, alone time may be as basic as watching television without interruption, or simply hanging out in the garage or getting on the computer. It could be a number of things to a man but often times it is not necessarily time alone to clean the house or run errands for a woman. A man's alone time needs to allow him peace on a level that women often don't experience. Apparently with men, alone time sometimes means not thinking. Alone time in that special void space that only men know how to access. There is a funny guy, Mark Gungor, who does an entire bit on the "nothing box" in a man's head. (Search "The Nothing Box, Mark Gungor" on the Internet for his hysterical YouTube Videos.) He talks about how men compartmentalize everything in their brain and cannot actually co-habit two areas of conflicting interest at the same time but that moreover there is a space for "nothing." He goes on to give examples about how if you ask a man what he's thinking and he says "nothing" then more than likely he really is thinking about absolutely nothing.

Women will rarely comprehend the idea of truly thinking about "nothing." Unless you are a lady who often meditates as a regular practice, you probably rarely shut it all off. We are like these beasts of thought that never shut down and even when we try to shut it off, thoughts constantly leak into our minds. In fact, for guys who don't already know this about women, we deserve to score some bonus points for this. Think about it if you are a man reading this. Can you imagine not ever being able to shut off your mind chatter to find any peace? Imagine, you are having sex and you think about doing the dishes. Or you are taking a shower and you cannot stop thinking of your "to do" list. Or you are trying to sleep and all you can do is think about work or that forgotten task that completely prevents you from falling into a dream state or deep sleep the entire night.

Men cannot likely imagine such a life of dwelling on so many details. It would probably be devastating to a man to lead such an existence of chaos and stress. Women usually do it every day of their lives. It may in fact account for the high level of prescription drug use we see amongst women who are in need of healthy down time but who continue instead to max out their stress levels.

There are effective ways for women to find the peace that alone time was meant to bring them if only they stop beating up on themselves long enough to find it. I bring up again meditation. This is a practice that has been proven to reduce stress. Another example might be going to the gym or going to the store and picking out a bouquet of flowers for no particular reason. Or it could be playing music, watching a good comedy or doing arts and crafts. Consider also free writing, yoga, swimming, running or simply laughing out loud. Whatever it is, all women should take time to figure out a form of relaxation that works for them and make it a priority in their lives. Every outlet should include consideration of the breath. Deep breathing can immediately lead to relaxation.

Since one of the biggest challenges for people in relationships is often in allowing others to take their alone time, most people should probably practice offering their partner some space. It seems to be against human nature to think of others first. We often do much of what we do with an expectation of something in return. Imagine for a moment that we truly put our loved ones first. Consider catering to your significant other's need for alone time so much so that you offer it to them. For most people it would come as a surprise if someone offered them some time alone. Speaking from personal experience some of my happiest moments have been when my husband said to me, "Honey, why don't you go get a massage or treat yourself to a pedicure. You deserve it. Would you like to do that right now?" I think just hearing those words put me into an instant trance.

If you're a woman, try saying to your man, "Babe, why don't you go take a little time to yourself to do that thing that you like to do and relax for a little while. I love you and just want you to know that you deserve it." Most guys would positively be shocked to hear that from a woman. They wouldn't believe their ears. For some of us, we think we give plenty of space to our loved ones but we neglect to acknowledge it. However, by addressing it as such you give the other person the peace of mind of knowing that you want them to relax because you love them. Be sure to clarify that it is because you feel they deserve it and not because you are trying to get rid of them. Try it. Offer some alone time to the person you love when they least expect it and see how grateful they are for your consideration of their needs. Honoring each other in this regard can add a new layer of peace to any relationship.

BEGIN WITH "YES, AND" TACTICS
- ALL OF LIFE IS AN IMPROV

"Some people misunderstand improv... It seems that improv is all about being funny. But it is not. Improv is about being spontaneous. It is about being imaginative. It is about taking the unexpected and then doing something unexpected with it... The key is to be open to crazy ideas and build on them..."

All of life is an improv. Moreover, every intimate relationship that you are in is also an improv. In order to keep the flow in a relationship it is particularly important to be creative and masterfully spontaneous. Beginning with "yes, and" rather than "no" is one of the most effective ways I've ever discovered to keep things peaceful and positive in my marriage. It does not require anyone to be right, and it simultaneously does not make anyone wrong.

Try saying this 10 times fast: "You're right..."

When it comes to communication in a relationship with someone you love there is no success that will ever come from trying to get the "win," so to speak, in an argument or disagreement. The problem is that when it comes to a relationship, you have no control over who decides to remember what and for how long. Though at times a heated discussion may ensue with your loved one, trying to feel smart or high and mighty by being right, will usually end in a loss for all.

Progressing through a disagreement with a loved one can be quite simple. This is in fact true for both men and women. Begin with "Yes, and..." or "You're right." Now practice with me. "Yes and..." "You're right." Good work. Oh wait, did you struggle with that exercise? Well, just keep reciting it like a mantra. If you master this simple exercise, you can change your life in ways that exceed your expectations. Truly, think about anytime in your life when you had an argument with someone and they proved you to be wrong. Did you suddenly like the other person more because they proved themselves right? Undoubtedly the answer to that is no. It is quite OK to express your opinion or point of view after starting with "yes and." For example, "Yes and I believe the dog could still use another walk. What do you think?" Or, "You're right, you did take him out several hours ago and I appreciate that. I think maybe it would be a treat if we took him out again." Proving another person wrong, especially a loved one, will not help to gain their respect and admiration. But accepting and acknowledging another person's point of view and then offering your own will disarm people and open people up to what you want to express. Remember the mantra. "Yes and..." Or, "You're right!"

SMILE

"Let us always meet each other with a smile, for the smile
is the beginning of love."
~ Mother Theresa

"If you have only one smile in you, give it to the people you love.
Don't be surly at home, then go out in the street and start grinning
'Good morning' to total strangers."
~ Maya Angelou

Smile and mean it! A man's greatest challenge is in pleasing his woman. In a moment of truth my husband said to me, "I like when you look at me..." then there was a pause and he started over and said, "I like my wife to look at me and smile." My husband wants a happy wife. That's it. Simple, right?! There is a fundamental need for a man to please his woman. This is what really makes a man a man. Why? Because there is no greater challenge. Men love a good challenge. But one of the greatest challenges in life will almost always be that of pleasing his woman. Seem ridiculous? Take a survey. Seriously, talk to every man you encounter and ask him how easy it is to please a woman. Ask any man married, "What's the secret to a happy marriage?" Listen to what he says. We've heard the sayings... "Happy wife, happy life." Or as Gilbert K Chesterton put it, "Marriage is an adventure, like going to war." Or as Sacha Guitry stated, "When a man steals your wife there is no better revenge than to let him keep her." And the most common answers, "compromise" and "she's always right."

Day to day life is already a challenge. Human beings are equipped to handle struggles and excitement, deep sadness and hurt, love and life. Often the most difficult times are when things become routine with<u>out</u> the excitement of "new" or "traumatic." How do you deal with monotony in your love life? This can be a time when you have the opportunity to grow by practicing the simplest of things such as smiling. When life becomes routine, motivation can fall short. It is then when we tend to most lack initiative and drive and become most depressed or stale. When things become routine in a relationship, you typically have extra time on your hands. This could be a great time to learn something new. Take a class. Plan a creative outing with the person you love or enjoy an ordinary meal and call it "special." Rather than turn to a common vice of drugs and alcohol or laziness, reach out and really make a special effort to change your routine in your love life. And again, smile.

When day to day life says to you, "This is it, everything you've worked for has led you here," count your blessings and make formal plans to shake things up in a beautiful way. Remember, you are exactly where you are supposed to be in this moment.

When your significant other makes you so mad, you could scream, instead, smile and remember that you have someone in your life. There's not a couple out there who doesn't at some point in a relationship make the other person extremely mad. What is it that allows another person to make us so mad? Let's stop for a moment and assume that the circumstances are irrelevant. In reality, the circumstances usually are irrelevant. It does not matter who you are or what the reason is, every human goes through a range of emotions. Our realities are all our own and our interpretations of everything around us are totally up to us. We all question things and we all have different buttons that can be pushed but we all have the buttons. What we each hold value in as being important varies from person to person.

What if we could stop holding on to stupid little pet peeves and just lighten up? Ponder for a moment what is going on from your partner's point of view anytime you feel that they are taking your needs for granted. When you consider another's point of view, you may find that the little annoyances suddenly hold less importance to you. This however, is a practice most of us have not mastered. It is a constant practice to let small annoyances go. Everything that emotionalizes you is based on your perspective. When you take the initiative to see things from other's perspectives, though you may not agree, you will soon see the reason people act the way they do. This is definitely true in love relationships. In many cases, what is going on with your significant other probably has absolutely nothing to do with you. The person you love is generally doing the best they can with what they know. Their tools are different from yours, just as you are operating to the best of your ability with what you know.

If you want to try a little exercise to help you smile more by letting go of small frustrations caused by the things your partner does, try this. Write down on a piece of paper all of the things that your partner does that really make you crazy. Then take each of those things and ponder how your significant other may potentially view those things. Ask yourself how your life would be different if you were to simply find a new way of looking at and dealing with those very items. Then shred them. Next, write down on a piece of paper everything that you do that makes your loved one crazy mad. Ask yourself, why these things are so frustrating to your partner. Then come up with a couple of ideas on how you can alleviate their frustration surrounding those things that you take for granted. Next implement those changes. Watch your life change. Watch as your partner's burdens are lifted. Then take all that energy and put it towards some fun. Get playful. Do something spontaneous. Do something out of your routine that's just plain kind.

Simple things are often profound. Write a note and leave it on the bathroom mirror that says "Man, you look good today." Or stick $5 in a card and say, "Coffee is on me." Just do something. Anything kind can change an entire course of a day and habits of such will completely change your life, fast! Then smile. Take a look at what is great in your life and smile about it. Double the amount of time you spend smiling and watch as your day to day existence comes to life and more importantly how the person you love begins to light up around you, because of you.

INSIGHTS

Alone Time

1. Everyone needs alone time.
2. For men, it's essential to have time to go into their cave.
3. Women may substitute alone time with "away" time.
4. There are many things a guy may do when he's taking alone time. The key is that women don't question it.
5. If a lady asks a guy what he's thinking about and he replies, "nothing," then there's a chance he really could be thinking about "nothing!"
6. It is very rare and often difficult for a woman to think about nothing.
7. There are effective ways for women to find peace with alone time through meditation and other practices.
8. The biggest challenge for people in relationships with regard to alone time is typically in granting it to their partner.
9. Try offering alone time to your partner and acknowledging it as such so that they know they are allowed to relax during that time. Spell it out for them that you actually want them to take some peaceful time to themselves.

Begin with "Yes, and" Tactics - All of Life is an Improv

1. All of life is an improv.
2. Begin with "Yes, and" rather than "No..." to allow communication to flow with ease.
3. There is no success to be gained from being right or from winning an argument, just for the sake of winning it, in any marriage or relationship.
4. Even while expressing your point of view you can begin a sentence with "You're right..." Then fill in whatever you have to say after it.

5. When you start with "no" in a conversation, it often starts the other person off on the defensive.
6. Beginning with "Yes, and" can be a powerful way to open people up to what you have to share, even if what you say following it, conflicts with their point of view.

Smile

1. To smile is to be beautiful.
2. Men want their women happy.
3. The greatest challenge for a man will nearly always be that of pleasing a woman. Seeing his woman smile will provide evidence that he is doing his job as a man.
4. Some of the most difficult times in a relationship can often be when things simply become monotonous.
5. During monotony, it is a perfect time to gain knowledge, learn something new and grow.
6. Anytime your loved one makes you mad, stop and smile with gratitude for the fact that you have them in your life.
7. Everyone's reality is their own. Your interpretation of everything is completely up to you.
8. What if you stopped holding on to the little things?
9. Ponder what is going on with your partner. From their point of view.
10. Come up with ways to alleviate your partner's frustration with some of the annoying things you do, by making small changes. Also try offering your perspective at a time when your partner is not charged with frustration.
11. Do something out of routine that is just plain kind, even something small. Simple things can be profound.
12. Double the amount of time you spend smiling.

8

When to Throw in the Towel

FAILURE

"I have not failed. I've just found 10,000 ways that won't work."
~ *Thomas A. Edison*

"If you believe yourself unfortunate because you have loved and lost, perish the thought. One who has loved truly, can never lose entirely."
~ *Napoleon Hill*

Love with all your might and never stop doing so. When you lose, you have still won by gaining knowledge, experience and the building materials for character. Most importantly, most very importantly, you have loved.

Everyone experiences failure. At some point in your life you have to fail. As long as you do, you can take it as a reminder that you are alive. At one time or another your failure will be in a relationship right when you most think you have mastered the art of dealing with people. You will come across someone who is impossible and unreasonable. Yes, you will meet someone who makes you feel like you have no control or as if you have slightly lost your mind. When it happens, they may make you want to pull your own hair out or want to hit things. Let me assure you. You are not crazy! This may be one of those times when perhaps you have made some mistakes but often times this is with someone with whom none of the rules, none of that advice you give or get, and none of your logical actions will work to win this person over to your way of thinking. Keep in mind when this happens that there is still potential but it is likely a time when you will need to step back and analyze what you really want in your life.

We have all heard of those people who in the beginning hated each other and even some who physically fought then ended up best friends or lovers. Maybe even you. The truth is that when people decide they are not going to make it easy on you, sometimes there is nothing that you can do on the side of kind persuasion to win them over to your way of thinking. Not in love or in friendships. Not until you have a knock-down, drag-out fight or you walk away and give up. I have always said that the only way to a liar's heart is with a lie and the only way to get through to an unreasonable person is to get unreasonable. This is one of those times when spelling it out does not seem to have an impact. Have faith as the fight is sometimes the very thing needed to get to the love at the core. Meanwhile, abandoning the need to hold on too tightly can simultaneously set you free.

Take a look at the people from your past that were unreasonable, and see if you can recall what you did to get through to them or what you did that never worked. Realize that your past can create a clear perspective of your future. Some of the most influential leaders and couples in the world first failed time and again before becoming an inspiration to others.

The fight is part of the journey. Sometimes part of your

success comes from going through the fighting and arriving on the other side, then clearing away the guilt and adding in forgiveness. Learn to fight without ego. No matter who you are, there will be a fight at some point in your life. Life just doesn't come without challenges. It's all part of the process.

Whenever there is a serious struggle in a love relationship there is always opportunity to grow from it. For instance, what if, you simply let go of your dedication to controlling the outcome of the next argument you had? What if you merely let go of your expectations for a moment? How hard would it then be? How long would a fight truly last? How much power would anyone have over you?

Consider this the next time you are trying to prove a point. What if you stopped and imagined that you were staring in a mirror, listening to your own judgments and opinions. Do you need to take some of your own advice? My husband and I make it a practice to always know in our own hearts that when others share their issues, it typically has more to do with them than anyone else. Now when we give each other advice we both start laughing as we always realize we more than likely need to take our own advice. We rarely then ever take anything personally. This quickly removes the majority of our judgments of others as well. This one practice has made all of our relationships stronger and more filled full of respect.

If you are with someone with whom you feel you cannot communicate with at this time, or you have been pursuing someone with whom you have felt powerless, remember this: Powerlessness in a relationship is in and of itself the ultimate POWER once you surrender to it! Failure to communicate is bound to happen at some point in your life. Failure should only encourage you to go deeper within to regain your own independent source of peace. From there can tap into greater depths of understanding that will allow you to become an even more effective communicator.

SUB-PAR RELATIONSHIPS

"If you don't love me, somebody will. If you're not missing me, somebody is. If you don't care about me, somebody does. You're replaceable."
~ Unknown

"Every adversity, every failure, every heartbreak, carries with it the seed of an equal or greater benefit."
~ Napoleon Hill

"Success is not final, failure is not fatal: It is the courage to continue that counts."
~ Winston S. Churchill

This may well be the hardest part of this book for me to write as it is fairly serious in nature.

A quick disclaimer: If you are being held in a relationship because you are scared for your life or for the lives of others who you know, this is not who this section is written for. For those of you in a situation as such, I pray you find help as soon as possible. There are also those who have settled, with very good intentions, to ensure their children are taken care of, or other similar situations. For those of you with complete heart and unselfishness behind your decision to accept sub-par circumstances in your relationship, this section is also not intended for you.

This section is specifically written for those people who know that they are in a relationship by choice where there is frequent abuse of personal boundaries or constant judgment by others who see only what they choose to see in the relationship. Usually this is a relationship where the line is often crossed by your partner of what is considered by you to be reasonable or right. We all have either been with this type of person or know or have known this type of person at some point in our lives.

There are lots of reasons why you might be in an imperfect or sub-par relationship. For the record, all relationships are imperfect. However, if you are someone who compared to the average Joe, seems to have settled for a seriously sub-par mate and you are struggling with how to handle it, the options are simple. Accept it, leave it, or complain about it. Nobody wants to hear the complaining part for more than a year or two maximum. Those of us in good relationships who really appreciate our partners do eventually tire of the complaining by those who do not have good relationships. The best thing you can do is realize you are now really down to two options. Accept it or leave it. OK, technically, you could throw in another option, "change it." However, the only thing you can really change is yourself. Typically by the time you are seeking advice on this subject you've probably made all the mistakes of allowing your boundaries to be crossed so many times that you are already stuck in a bad way. If you're cringing as you begin to read this section, (you know who you are) you've probably settled for someone who does not in the eyes of others meet all of your needs in a way that some people feel you deserve.

I am a big believer that no two people stay together without balance. Therefore, you may be treated badly in one regard while you are treated better than most in another. In other words, what the rest of us see is only part of the story. Even in many abusive relationships where the victim stays in it by choice, in many cases, there is more going on than meets the eye. Typically there is something that both people are getting from the relationship to keep them both involved with each other. This is not *always* the case, but very often it is. Again, when people continue to be in relationships by choice, where they are not treated as well as others think they should be, they are in fact getting something out of the relationship that keeps them coming back. When people cease to get that thing that they need which balances the negative, they will move on.

A seemingly sub-par relationship typically has certain fundamental commonalities. To begin with this type of relationship is often tumultuous or passionate on some level. The passion and excitement, even when negative in nature, can cause chemical releases in the brain that are stimulating. These stimulants in fact are addicting and often explain to some degree why people continue going back time and again for more of the same in a relationship such as this. Though often unhealthy in the long run, these relationships can be highly adrenalizing or arousing to people. If you are someone who knows you are currently settling for certain aspects of a relationship that do not live up to your ideals, in exchange for a little adrenaline rush, you may already realize you are doing this to some degree. For example, if your partner insults you with cruel words in exchange for a bouquet of flowers when he or she makes up, you may have decided that this is an equal trade for the negativity you put up with and therefore, you accept it.

Some people in relationships such as the aforementioned types truly are ready to make a change. That said they may be finding it difficult to pull away from their addiction to the relationship, much like someone who may be addicted to substance abuse or gambling. They truly need assistance to break away. Keep in mind, nobody in this type of relationship leaves it without first making up their mind that they are ready for the change. If you happen to be a friend or family member of someone in a situation such as what I am describing, the greatest gift you can give your loved one, usually, is unconditional love and acceptance. People in these types of relationships often have to first admit that they have a problem, or decide that they personally need a change before they can be helped.

If you are someone who is in this situation and you are not trying to get out of it, in fact you are quite content to have the high highs and low lows in your life, then you might need to work on the acceptance of those aspects of the relationship which you loathe. That could be a partner cheating or spending too much time at a race track or numerous other possibilities that simulate crossing the line for you. Sometimes the unacceptable behaviors that drive you to complain may be as simple as their lack of affection, or unexplained absences, or even simply ongoing rude and bossy manors. All of these behaviors are usually balanced by make-up affection, sincere and loving words, very personal attention or sometimes simply gifts and money. I don't mean to sound redundant, but there is something that keeps a person in this type of relationship that is balancing the negativity that the rest of the world is witnessing. Some of this may be resolved by better spelling out boundaries after a person has worked on their self-esteem but often the perpetuated situation is habitual.

Let's talk about what's right and wrong for a moment. This line is very different for each individual. Everyone on earth has different boundaries. We all have ways to find common threads of truth for what is acceptable through society, through church, friends, family, etc., but I'm not sure if anyone has all the answers on this. Humans love the act of judging as it helps us all to make ourselves feel better about our own circumstances. Yet only you can decide what is right or wrong for you personally.

If you are someone who is living in a tumultuous relationship and you continually go back and forth between loving and hating the person you are with, and you have not yet made a choice on how it should play out, I recommend that you consider making a list of all of your ideal traits in a partner. The very first step in helping to make a decision is in addressing the way things currently are and comparing it to what you really want. Go through your list and circle every trait that your partner has. Then make a list of all the traits you feel you cannot live with forever that your partner has. Reflect on what you are seeing and listen to your gut instincts about whether or not this is the person you want to have in your life forever. If you decide this person is someone you can't live without and you cannot change the behaviors that make you nuts, the answer is simple. Accept them.

If you are unwillingly sharing your significant other with another person, meaning they are spending time with someone other than you, and you are not pleased about it, nor can you change it, yet everything else in your being is telling you to stick it out with this person, simply accept the circumstances. You can only change that which is within your control. Therefore, if you cannot change your partner's decision about another person, then all you can do is decide what you can personally do for yourself, while your partner is off with that person. This other person could potentially be a lover or it could be an in-law, or a parent of your significant other's child, or anyone else for that matter.

If you are choosing to stick it out with someone who is considered sub-par by you or others, there are many things you can do to improve your self-confidence and to gain personal power. Work out and learn something new or spend time with friends and family, and so on. The key is to occupy your time with those things which make you a better person while they are off committing whatever crimes they are committing. This way if you ever change your mind and decide you are no longer going to accept your partner's actions, you will be more than strong enough to walk away.

If you are currently trying to change your circumstances or get out of your situation, and are simply too weak to say "no" to your partner's charm when they turn it on, you may need to make a tough decision. Are you serious about changing your circumstances? If you are serious about making a change and you have simply not found the way to do it, it may be time to run your own intervention. This may require something as drastic as a move or as simple as taking a personal empowerment course. Start by feeding yourself some inspiration and then get tough. If you consider yourself an addict then take a look at the discipline it takes some people to quit their addictions. Start your own twelve step program. Make it up. Write it down. Begin where you are. Take even a small step towards your own recovery and begin by putting one foot in front of the other. Soon enough you'll be marching out the door.

WHEN THROWING IN THE TOWEL
MAKES SENSE

"When one door of happiness closes, another opens;
but often we look so long at the closed door that we do not see the one
which has been opened for us."
~ Helen Keller

"The only thing we have to fear is fear itself."
~ Franklin D. Roosevelt

There are times when you know on a gut level that you are in a relationship (love or friendship) with someone who is <u>not</u> right for you. You know deep inside that this is not someone you want in your life. Sometimes we are in love with this person while other times we are not. Sometimes these people are good people and sometimes they are not. Either way the end result is inevitable. You know that they are not someone you want intimately in your life forever regardless of what others say to you about them, and regardless of what they say or do directly to you. This section is for you if you are currently with, have ever been with or could possibly ever be with somebody who you do <u>not</u> want to be with forever.

Life is extremely precious. Sometimes it's too short. And your death date is both unpredictable and non-negotiable. What would keep anyone with someone who brings them down in life? The answer may be kids, money, a house and possibly a hundred other solid excuses and sometimes all of the above. The bottom line is they have fear. We all have fear. The reality is some of us are actually with a person we DO KNOW we want to be with forever and we still have fear. However, those of us who know we are with "the one," will be working through our fears with the person we'd like to spend eternity with. Others may need to work on transitioning out of their current situation.

Let's quickly validate if you are with a person at this time who you do not want to spend eternity with (most of you already know who you are). Ponder these questions. Then close your eyes put your hand on your heart and ask yourself these same questions again in silence. Be completely open to the answers that come to you. If you begin to cry, allow it to flow. If you have spent a tremendous amount of time with this person, if you have a superb amount of baggage with this person, still open yourself to accept the truth of your gut feelings as they flow through you providing you with an undeniable answer.

Validation questions...

1. If you were told today that you would die tonight, is this person, the person you would want by your side?
2. If you were dependent and required 24-7 care, would this person care for you?
3. If this person required 24-7 care, would you commit yourself to them fully?
4. Do you want to grow old with this person?
5. Does this person make you laugh?
6. Can you be yourself completely with this person?
7. Do you trust this person with your life?
8. Are you in love with or do you love this person on a spiritual level?
9. Do you forgive this person completely when they make mistakes?
10. Does this person make everything else in your life worth-while?

After completing the validation questions, if you answered yes to every question above, you are with "a keeper." If you did this exercise and do not have a gut level instinct one way or another or were unable to answer some of the questions, you may not yet be in a position to make this determination. If you are someone who knows undeniably that this is not someone you should be with, you can begin making your plans to "throw in the towel." This type of transition is not a shameful act. For those of you who guilt yourselves, I'm suggesting to you that you let go of guilt for this period of your life's transformation and create what I call your "out plan." Your "out plan" is simply your strategic plan for changing your circumstances.

Prolonging the inevitable is quite common. However, it is not necessary to draw out these transitions as long as many of us do. Though often requiring a thought-out approach to your big life change, the key is remembering that what's best for you is best for everybody involved. This is not selfish. When you hold on to someone for the wrong reasons, you not only hold back yourself but you hold back the person who you are with, who needs to be released as well. The greatest inspiration comes from those people who are willing to live out their lives truthfully. Everyone including myself is in awe of someone who seemingly risks it all to do what is truthful and right for them personally. This person is not egotistical. They are setting everyone free. Children are also set free by the truth. Children are a great example to all of us for how to live a truthful life. They are free spirited and are honest by nature.

Children can immediately tell you the truth while adults get stuck calculating everything to a fault. People frequently neglect their own heart in an attempt to do what they think is right for others. Yet the right thing is nearly always to follow your own heart. I do not mean this from an impulsive sense, rather from the standpoint of merely living a truthful life. When you do what is right for you it sets everyone else free to do what's right for them and everyone grows exponentially. Children want what is best for their parents and they do not do what they are told to, they do what they SEE their parents doing even from a young age. They learn by example and are much more resilient than people give them credit for. If you are a parent and living a lie for the purpose of your children, I simply offer you this. Consider who you really want to be for your children. This is not intended to suggest that you should take any particular action.

As a mother it is my goal to do whatever it takes to have an amazing relationship with my daughter's father and I'm lucky and grateful I have a husband who is willing to do the same. My hope is that I set the best example I can for my daughter with how to be in a healthy relationship, so that she draws healthy boundaries for herself with whomever she one day attracts in love.

If you do not have children and you are considering "throwing in the towel" it is possible your situation may be a bit less complicated. Yet, you may have many other complications. Usually if you are with someone you do not want to be with, it is in fact due to complications, many of which may be fear based living solely in your imagination. When you are scared or hurting, the key is to open your heart wider. Then and only then will you fully move through whatever it is and get past the fear with the most complete possible healing you can have.

When it's time to throw in the towel, be forgiving of yourself and forgiving of others and remember, that there is no need to guilt others or be driven by guilt. Being true to yourself is admirable and is always best for everyone involved. If you need to make an "out plan," do it, make the change happen, and begin your life! Making a transition out of a relationship is often filled with drama, but drama does not have to affect you or drive your actions. You can allow the story to be what it is and simply be driven by the choices that help you begin your life with new circumstances. Lastly, there need be no excuse or reason that you have to explain to make a change in a relationship, if you simply know you are not with the person you believe you should be with forever. You can walk away without a story and allow others to go through their own grieving process without your guidance. Your job is not to solve other people's feeling issues but instead to do what is best for you, to free others to do what is best for them.

IF YOU LOVE SOMEONE SET THEM FREE

*"If you love something let it go. If it comes back to you, it's yours forever.
If it doesn't, then it was never meant to be."*
~ Unknown

*"What the caterpillar calls the end of the world,
the master calls a butterfly."*
~ Richard Bach

We've all heard some rendition of the saying, "If you love something set it free." Enough already. Yah, yah, we know that's what we are supposed to do, right? Let's deal with how to really make that happen. The sooner you practice this level of trust, which few of us possess as a natural virtue, the sooner you will be living in a much deeper state of peace. Truly nobody owns anyone. Not you, nor I, nor anyone on earth. The truth is that even if you are legally married and have 10 children together you still don't own the person you married. We'd like to think that we do at times, but we do not! The reality is love is all giving. True love is acceptance and trust. Trust should not be confused with trustworthy in this case. I'm referring only to the act of having trust that love will live on, regardless of circumstances.

Now what to do to give your heart over to the level of trust that allows you to set someone free, completely and fully. This requires a kind of trust, love, release and acceptance that allows you to fully breathe into the possibility that you may never get to be with this particular person again ever, and the trust that you will live and love again. Moreover that you will have this person or someone better. The true allowance for the possibility that there may in fact be someone better for you can empower you, but usually doesn't make letting go of someone much easier. Let's face it, when people are telling you this, it ranks up there with the saying, "There are plenty of fish in the sea." Equally annoying and usually at a time when we most need to be reassured that the person we love will continue to love us as much as we do them.

Here's the deal. Know that if you are having to make the decision to trust in the release of someone you love, it's OK to let that someone go. You are making the right decision. Better to practice this before you are in the position of heartbreak, I realize. If you are in the midst of a serious heartache, heartbreak or a jealous attack, just know the very best thing on earth you can truly do for yourself and your own personal worth, value and sex appeal, is in fact, to let go!

If you are walking away from someone who doesn't love you as you deserve, letting go begins by seeing yourself as worthy enough to do this very thing. In other words, you have to visualize yourself as good enough to walk away, and expect a person that you love to still desire and want you. The alternative would be that you are potentially with someone who really does not want to be with you. Therefore, they are living a lie and so are you. Who wants to be with someone who doesn't want to be with them? I don't! I want to know that without a shadow of a doubt the person I'm with would rather be with me than anyone else on earth. Otherwise, I'd recommend that they go be where they want to be and free me to find someone who loves me the way I deserve to be loved. None-the-less, I get that this is easier said than done. This practice of raising your own self-worth is not one of choice but one of necessity if you are in a position of needing to let go of someone you love. You must know without a shadow of a doubt that you are worthy. You are special. You are one of a kind and there is no one else on earth that brings what you bring to the table. Stand up or sit up tall and lift your spirits to a place where you realize that you are completely in control of your worthiness of love. You are beautiful, sexy and a gift to someone who chooses you.

The beauty of the act of letting someone go is that it's not your job to convince someone to see you a certain way. If your struggle is in trying to convince someone to hold you in a higher regard, just know, that the absolute hottest thing you can do for the person you are crazy about is to let them go. Yes, you heard that right. If you want to increase the hot factor, all you need to do is let them go, and the universe will deliver up the message directly to the person you are letting go, through an energetic express mail delivery system. Watch as you receive a call, text or email. You have to really make the decision that this is what you are doing mind you. You can't just pretend. Truth is, you're better off to fake it than not. But everyone picks up on energy. If you're someone who has pulled the "I'm leaving you" card in an attempt to get a person's attention prior to this attempt but didn't really mean it, you'll have to do a better job of truly making your mind up that you're letting them go once and for all. Until you do this, this person will not realize what they've lost. Once you do, however, the majority of the time the person you are letting go will pick up on the energy and suddenly take notice of you and make an asserted effort not to lose you. It does at times require patience but wait and you will see the truth in this.

In the end what matters is that you know that you will love and be loved again by this person or someone better. You simply need to trust in the process of love. Know that love will come your way. Love happens. In fact, there's no stopping it. However, holding on to someone out of fear does not increase the amount of love you receive nor does it ensure that love will happen. It has the opposite effect. The greatest power comes from love combined with trust. Love fueled by knowing. The act of love combined with knowing will deliver you your greatest desires. Set people free and great things will come your way.

INSIGHTS

Failure

1. Everyone experiences failure.
2. There is always potential for something great, even in failure. When you experience failure it is a time to analyze what you really want in your life.
3. The only way to get through to an unreasonable person is more than likely to get unreasonable.
4. Your past can create a clear perspective of your future.
5. Powerlessness is in and of itself the ultimate POWER once you surrender to it!
6. Abandoning the need to hold on can give you complete freedom.
7. In the end, without struggles, who would you be?
8. The fight is part of the journey.
9. Learn to fight without ego.
10. No matter who you are, there will be a fight. Life doesn't come without challenges.
11. Let go of your dedication to controlling the outcome and life's challenges will no longer have power over you.

Sub-Par Relationships

1. All relationships are imperfect.
2. If you have settled for a seriously sub-par mate and you are struggling with how to handle your situation, the options are simple. Accept it, leave it, or complain about it.
3. No two people stay together without balance.
4. When you cease to get that thing that you need which balances the negativity, you will move on.
5. Passion and excitement, even when negative in nature, can cause chemical releases in the brain that are stimulating and addicting.

6. Most people in addictive relationships are unable to be helped by an outside party unless they first make up their minds to make a change themselves.
7. The line for what is right or wrong for each individual is different from the next. Everyone has different boundaries.
8. Everyone judges everyone else but only you can decide what is right for you.
9. If you have decided that you want to stay with a person who you are currently with who has some bad habits or issues that you can't stand, accept them. Remember you've decided to stay.
10. If you have decided you are with someone who you do not choose to be with forever, begin your own twelve-step program to change your circumstances.

When Throwing in the Towel Makes Sense

1. There are times in life when people end up with people that they do not want to be with forever. The knowing is on a gut level.
2. If you know you want to make a transition away from someone who is not right for you, there is no reason to delay the decision. Life is short.
3. Living a lie for children does not necessarily serve them.
4. There are ways to validate if you are with someone who you should stay with or leave. Ask validation questions to help ensure your heart is making decisions that are not based in fear or guilt.
5. When it's time to throw in the towel, be forgiving of yourself and forgiving of others. Remember that there is no need to guilt anyone or to be driven by guilt.
6. If you need to make an out plan, do it and make the change happen and begin your life!
7. Drama does not have to affect you or drive your actions.

8. There need be no excuse or reason that you have to explain to make a change in a relationship if you simply know that you are not with the person you want to be with forever.
9. Doing what is best for you will set others free to do what is best for them as well.

If You Love Someone Set Them Free

1. If you love someone set them free.
2. Love is all giving.
3. True love is acceptance and trust.
4. You will live and love again.
5. You will have this person or someone better.
6. There are plenty of fish in the sea. It's true.
7. If you need to trust in the release of someone you love, it's OK.
8. The best thing you can do for yourself and your own personal worth, value and sex appeal is in fact to let go!
9. Letting go begins with seeing yourself as worthy enough to let go and knowing that you will have love.
10. You are one of a kind and there is no one else on earth who is like you.
11. You are a gift to someone who chooses you.
12. The absolute hottest thing you can do for the person you are crazy about is let them go. If you want to increase the hot factor, all you need to do is let go.
13. Everyone picks up on energy. Eventually if you want to get your message across that you have in fact let someone go, you have to truly let them go.
14. Know that you will love again.
15. It's not your job to decide how love will happen.
16. Trust in the process of love and know that it will come your way.
17. The greatest power comes from love fueled by knowing and love combined with trust.

9

Hurt, Open, Heal, Open

ON HURT – THE FASTEST WAY TO HEAL

"The wound is the place where the Light enters you."
~ Rumi

"If you're going through hell, keep going."
~ Winston Churchill

When your heart is hurting, the fastest way to heal is to OPEN YOUR HEART WIDER STILL into the pain and it will quickly pass through you triggering the beginning of the healing process.

Being honest with yourself is the first step to healing a broken heart. Healing begins with accepting what is, and more importantly accepting and forgiving any of your own mistakes if you feel you have made them. Realizing and remembering that you cannot change other people is critical. You only have control over yourself. You are a new person in this very moment right now from whomever you were a moment ago. And if you decide to be profoundly different now than a moment ago still, you can be that new person too. The challenge is in accepting that others may not see you as a new person right away. It takes persistence in being the new you in order that others may at some point recognize it. Your personal growth is not about other people's opinions. It is your process to go through, learn from, and blossom from.

Hurt is neither easy nor fun and hurt should not be cured by way of a pill. The most effective treatment for heartache is the act of feeling fully. It is said that emotion is "energy in motion." The act of an emotion being fully felt and experienced will result in the passing of that same feeling much more effectively than if it were squashed or contained in an attempt to appear strong or avoid embarrassment. Emotion comes in waves, and if allowed to live out fully, will move through you quickly. This will result in healing.

It is important to also be aware that there are many ways you can change your state of mind and the way you feel. About the time when it is the hardest to take action is when it is usually most important, to do that very thing. Try finding anything that can quickly pull you out of sadness. For example, play "happy" music or watch "feel good" films. Be with friends and family. Work out or take a walk. Be in nature. Help other people or animals. Volunteer. Write. Sing. Dance. Garden. Meditate. Eat healthy foods. Laugh for no reason at all. If all else fails, jump up and down and scream out loud! And certainly, most certainly cry out loud!

No one can discount the experience of sadness. It is the toughest state to break out of but can be one of the most empowering states for growth. When you commit to becoming a stronger and more loving person, and dedicate yourself to changing the way you feel when you are in a funk, you will quickly heal. The goal is to get through it without dwelling. Numbness is neither healthy nor a cure. Nor will bitterness protect you or make you a better person. Being brave enough to open yourself up wider to fully experience what is happening so that you can quickly let it pass is admirable and inspiring.

When it comes to hurt, be brave and be kind. These things will heal you.

SUICIDE – COMBATING GUILT TRIPS

"Take two aspirin and call me in the morning."
~ Unknown

I dialed a suicide hotline after an ex-boyfriend said he was going to commit suicide if I didn't come to see him. I was told to tell him that I'd call him in two weeks and then hang up and not pick up his calls. The point was to give him something to look forward to in the case that he truly was considering suicide, and still stop the cycle of manipulation that was being used to guilt me into returning to him. Many people fain suicide to get attention. If unsure in this type of situation, however, be sure to seek professional advice.

I had another ex-boyfriend who got so depressed he carved my initials in his hand with a knife and threatened suicide. I remember another time still, with yet another boyfriend, when I had to run for my car as fast as I could and take off before he would jump in front of my car. The stories go on. Fortunately, all of my exes are alive and well today and all are still dear friends. Depression and heartache can drive sane people to do insane things.

If you have needs that are vital to your health and happiness and you address those needs, it is usually best for everyone around you regardless of what you think others might think about it. Let me give you a somewhat random example related to combating guilt trips. Last night my baby sister was talking about how she was being guilt tripped into visiting our parents on the weekend. She hadn't seen her man in two weeks and he would arrive home on the weekend. She was truly dreading having to go stay at our parents for a couple days to please them, though she surely would love to see them on a different weekend. I pointed out a simple fact. If she went to see our parents when she'd rather be at home, she would end up being there wishing that she was elsewhere. Yet if she told our parents "Ah, man, I can't make it this week but I will be there next month." Then our parents would HAVE to accept it and they would look forward to her visit a month later, releasing the immediate pressure. In addition, she would be happy to visit a month later and she would not be wishing that she were somewhere else when she did it. My sister quickly had an "ah ha" moment and agreed that they would not continue to be upset if she just set the record straight quickly on her intentions and if she simply spoke her truth.

Here's another example of how what's good for you is good for everyone. Let's take the case of a good friend of mine who is sleeping with a "nice guy." She is not happy about it and does not consider it good sex but thinks the guy is such a nice guy that she feels guilty to walk away from him. Here's the issue. If she is not likely to develop an attraction to the guy but is clearly leading him on, who is going to win? Nobody. It would be better to break this guy's heart quickly and free him to go meet a more compatible match, simultaneously freeing her to find someone she is more attracted to. In the end, everyone wins. The flip is true as well. Ask yourself, "Do I want to be with someone who isn't into me but who continues to stay with me out of guilt?" No way! I sure hope not anyway. Since there are truly unlimited people on the planet, you can choose one that meets your needs from attraction to treatment. You just have to know that they are out there and open your heart.

Guilt trips are usually self-imposed. If you personally feel guilty at this time, begin by forgiving yourself. Trust in the idea that what is best for you is best for everyone involved. Allow yourself to gain perspective. Guilt trips are an unnecessary way of life.

CHANGING UNWANTED PATTERNS

"Where is the remote? All the way over there... Guess I'm watching this."
~ *Unknown*

*"Discipline: The missing link between the life you have
and the life you want."*
~ *Timber Hawkeye, Buddhist Boot Camp*

Everything in life is either new or old, usual or unusual, getting better or getting worse, a pattern or not. You know what is routine for you. You know those times when you said something and you felt bad that you said it, but you knew way before you spoke, that you were going to say it. You knew it was against your better judgment. You knew you shouldn't open your mouth, but you couldn't help yourself. Life is a series of patterns and sometimes your habits or patterns are not the best thing for you. Good habits are a plus but bad habits perpetuate themselves. Think of those times when you knew you were getting upset about something that someone was doing, but from an out of body perspective you were aware that it was ridiculous. You were hoping you wouldn't express yourself on the subject as you knew you would feel guilty right after, and then you did it anyway. These are the types of patterns I'm referring to. Knowing you shouldn't do or say something yet lacking the discipline to control your own impulses anyway.

So let's cut to the solution. Tony Robbins and countless others have given great techniques for breaking patterns such as pinching yourself every time you go to do something stupid. I've used and heard of other techniques like having a rubber band around your arm and snapping it every time you go to smoke for example. These types of techniques are options that are available to all of us. I personally used to hand my phone off at the bar to my girlfriends so that they would not allow me to call or "drunk-dial" my now husband, who I was irrationally in love with at the time. If I went to grab the phone back from whoever had it, I would step on my own foot to remind me to leave it alone. Soon enough I stopped reaching for it.

What if you just stopped in that moment, when you were about to do something you knew better than to do, and you replaced whatever you were about to say or do with a moment of silence? Really stop and think about it for a minute. Call it a moment to breathe, a moment to stop the brain's cycle, a moment to make a strategic change. Consider it a chance to make a life changing difference in your own patterns. This is certainly a practice that I, being the outspoken girl who cannot keep her mouth shut at times, needs to practice. I used to tell my dad, "If you have a comment that is followed by a criticism, say only the first sentence then THINK the rest of what you were going to say rather than speak it." He has gotten better over the years at keeping himself out of trouble with this technique.

Taking a moment or pausing can actually change your life for the better. For instance, for a woman who wants to hook up with a guy in the heat of the moment, but who simultaneously wants to gain the guy's respect, taking a moment to gain her composure can be the one thing that helps her to make a critical decision such as to withhold sex. A moment can give someone a chance to harness willpower. Again this starts by taking a moment to use good judgment.

If your lack of willpower is in the area of phoning, texting or emailing a potential partner, remember that you reduce sexual tension and lessen the attraction just a little bit each time you over-contact someone. Use discipline and remember once you hit send, you cannot pull it back. And every time you over explain the last thing you said, you again reduce attraction. Allowing things to just sit, with discipline to control your own mind's story about what another person is doing can give you tremendous power. We often think we know what another person feels or how they may respond to something we do or say. Yet, how can we know?

If you are someone who can't control your own phoning, texting and emailing, try channeling those impulses into more productive actions such as walking away from your electronics and/or meditating. If at first your willpower is lacking, start by stepping on your own foot or pinching yourself if you have to, to create a reminder trigger. Soon you will remember to pause for a moment to allow time for better decision making. In the end, if it is difficult to do then you know you are probably doing the right thing!

INSIGHTS

On Hurt – The Fastest Way to Heal

1. The fastest way to heal is to OPEN WIDER STILL into the pain.
2. Be honest with yourself.
3. Accept what is. Accept and forgive yourself if you feel you have made mistakes.
4. You cannot change other people.
5. You only have control over yourself. You are a new person in this very moment right now from who you were a moment ago. You can change from moment to moment if you want to.
6. If you've made changes to empower yourself, accept it if others don't notice the new you at first. It often takes time.
7. One of the most effective treatments for heartache is the act of feeling fully. Allowing emotion to move freely helps the emotion to pass.
9. Neither numbness nor bitterness help the healing process.
10. When it comes to hurt, be brave and be kind. Open your heart wider.

Suicide - Combating Guilt Trips

1. If you have needs that are vital to your health and happiness and you address them, it is typically best for everyone.
2. When you agree to spend time with someone who you don't want to be with, out of guilt, it holds back all parties involved.
3. Ask yourself if you would want anyone to stay with you out of guilt alone?
4. Free yourself and others if the time you spend with each other is not mutually desired.

Changing Unwanted Patterns

1. Everything in life is either new or old, usual or unusual, getting better or getting worse, a pattern or not.
2. Life is a series of patterns and sometimes your habits or patterns are not the best thing for you.
3. If you want to change something, stop and think about it for a minute. Call it a moment to breathe – a moment to stop the brain's cycle. A moment to make a transition. A life's change.
4. If you lack willpower in the area of phoning, texting or emailing a potential partner, remember that you reduce sexual tension and lessen the attraction just a little bit each time you over contact someone. Practice discipline.
5. With respect to obsessive texting and phoning, every time you over explain the last thing you said, you again reduce attraction. Allow things to just sit, with discipline to control your own mind's story about what another person may be doing or thinking.
6. Channel impulses into more productive actions such as working out, walking away from your electronics and/or meditating.
7. When it comes to discipline, if it is difficult to do then you know you are doing the right thing!

10

Attitude, Gratitude Makes Your Life

FIXING OTHER PEOPLE

"There is no respect for others without humility in one's self."
~ Henri Frederic Amiel

*"I claim to be a simple individual liable to err like any other fellow mortal.
I own, however, that I have humility enough to confess
my errors to retrace my steps."*
~ Mahatma Gandhi

I had an interesting conversation with an acquaintance today. He went on to tell me about the drama happening in his home. We had both just arrived at breakfast and he told me that he had to leave his house to escape the madness where moments before his wife (soon-to-be ex-wife) had just abruptly left the house and slammed the door on everyone in the house

153

including her own family who was visiting. They filed for divorce the week before and had not yet told their five children. He insisted it was mutually agreed upon and long overdue. He went on to explain that they had been sticking it out for their children up to this point.

The night before his twin sons had graduated from high school and all the family (in-laws) were in town. He had been trying to tell his wife for some time (twenty years that they'd been married) that she had been neglecting the family, even her own kids by making her job a priority to a fault. I asked him to tell me more.

He went on, "She is one of these people who cannot put her phone down for anything. If it rings it does not matter where she is, she has to answer it. She is constantly texting and won't look up at me or anyone else, even at a restaurant. She insists that her job is 24-7 and she has to do this to provide for the family, etc." (Both of them work and share expenses.) "I tell her that it can wait. That she can call someone back even if its 15 minutes later, they'll live. She can't stand it when I tell her anything. We get into huge fights over it but she can't see what she is doing."

I let him go on for a good 20 minutes about what a terrible wife and mom this lady was for being obsessed with her work. By the way you might be wondering right about now if this woman's work is curing cancer. Her 24-7 job is that of a restaurant manager.

This acquaintance of mine tells me how even his wife's own family has told him that she needs to relax when it comes to work and she has become edgy and snaps at the drop of a hat. When this acquaintance of mine finally told his wife that even her own brothers and parents agreed that she was too obsessed with her work, it lead to a confrontation and she quickly put her family on the spot to discuss it, at which time they denied the accusations. However, this particular day was finally the day, post sons' graduation that they all decided to come clean. They decided to tell her what she was doing (an intervention of sorts) leading to the eventual blow-up and slammed door, at which time the woman decided the best way to spite them for not understanding and for not appreciating her, was to go to work on her day off! I'm sure that showed them.

I said to this man, "Does your wife do anything well?" He could not answer at first so I got more specific. "Is your wife kind to your kids?"

He said, "Yes, sometimes but she snaps a lot."

I went on, "Do you know what's on her mind or what she worries about day in and day out?"

He said, "She worries about work." Then he started on a new tangent about how his wife gets angry at him for not cleaning the house and he believes he picks up all the time. "I just don't go around pointing it out every time I do it like she does," he explained.

C'mon, we can all relate to this story if we've ever lived with anyone other than ourselves.

So perhaps a mouthful of things that make you go "hmm" in this true story. Here's what I personally heard as this acquaintance of mine went on about his soon-to-be ex-wife's issues. "Waaah wahh waaah waahhhh.... Wahh WAAAAAH, waaah, Waaa! I've got issues."

As an intense observer of human beings when I hear people criticizing others, I especially hear the complainer's issues coming out. I couldn't help but think to myself during this rant, that this woman must be getting a significant feeling of importance from her job. This woman's job must make her feel so important that she is willing to sacrifice even time with her very own kids for it. He validated this further when he shared with me how his wife's job awarded her with "employee of the year" status but with <u>no raise</u> and it inspired her to work even harder. He could not understand why she was so seemingly over committed to her job.

The biggest recurring question I had to ask myself while hearing this rant about his wife was, "Why was it so important to this man to criticize and change his soon to be ex-wife's behavior or beliefs?" I wondered to myself, why a man who had already filed divorce papers was so intent on proving this woman wrong. What was it in his mind that made him feel the need to have this woman see his point of view and what was this need he had to get this woman to spend her time the way he was dictating it should be spent. Did he not realize that if he simply accepted this woman's behaviors including her annoying text habits, long hours and inability to focus on him, that suddenly she would find him more interesting and automatically feel compelled to pay more attention to him? How was it that I was the only one who could see this, I wondered internally. Then I heard my own issues arising in my silent analysis of his behavior. Oh, yes. That's right. Even I needed to be more accepting and willing to witness this man's path as he was spiraling down it without feeling the compelling need to advise him. After all I had to remind myself, he hadn't actually asked for my advice.

As human beings, we crave the feeling of importance. We need to feel appreciated more than almost any other emotion we can feel. There are stories everywhere you look, in the present and throughout history that prove the magnificent things that people will do for appreciation over what they will do for money. The "acquaintance" story is an example of where everyone is feeling a desperate desire for appreciation. Rather than showing their appreciation, both parties continually point out the faults in one another in an incessant failing effort to gain appreciation. In the end, you can clearly see, this did not work out for them as shown by their divorce.

It's unfortunate but true that as I write this section I recognize how I myself have a habit of criticizing my husband. This situation with this acquaintance is a bold reminder of the importance of changing the habit of criticism. Rather than trying to fix others by pointing out their annoying habits or faults, try finding the things you appreciate? Easier said than done? Of course it is at first. Practice is what creates a habit. As an experiment I invite you to find something GOOD in the next person you have the instinct to criticize. Then point it out. Be a witness to your own experiment and watch how it changes everything. Witness how your positive reinforcement of something good changes not only your own feelings but also how it changes the other person's behavior who you were initially feeling compelled to criticize. Then if you feel that a behavior still needs to be changed, perhaps consider finding another way to make a difference.

An alternate possibility for my acquaintance...

What if this guy had simply decided to praise his wife for her commitment to her job? What if he had acknowledged her efforts to create security for their family? What if he had decided to mention to his wife how he had a tremendous amount of gratitude for the quality time she spent with the kids when she was able to make the time with them? What if he had recognized that her job demanded a remarkable amount of her attention? And what if he had decided to be impressed by her high level of integrity and commitment to the company she had worked for as opposed to the alternative point of view which he had committed himself to for the prior twenty years. Would she have been more open to receiving his messages and would she have considered paying more attention to her husband and children? My guess is that a simple willing change in approach may have changed everything for them.

OTHER PEOPLE'S ATTITUDES

"There are things known and there are things unknown, and in between are the doors of perception."
~ *Aldous Huxley, English Novelist and Critic*

"Attitude is a little thing that makes a big difference."
~ *Winston Churchill*

A woman in her fifties with a sour look on her face at the grocery store CUTS YOU OFF with her full grocery basket, stepping in front of you as you are standing in a long checkout line. You have less than five items in your handheld basket and someone is waiting for you in a car in the parking lot. You have a giant thing of paper towels at your feet which you are pushing forward with your foot as you move slowly through the line. You are also holding on to two large jugs of orange juice in your other hand. The woman who cuts you off in line does NOT look up at you, nor acknowledge that you were clearly in front of her, already standing in line. You were simply trying to give plenty of distance between you and the next person in front of you, as a courtesy.

What is your immediate reaction? How do you feel? What do you do or say if anything while standing in line? What is going through your mind and how does your body feel?

Finally after what seems like forever, you get near the front of the line watching this woman as she fumbles through her purse looking for exact change. The woman then pulls out a coupon she wants applied to a wrong item which requires that the clerk call over a manager. Suddenly, she changes her mind about paying with cash and pulls out her checkbook with no regard for you still standing behind her.

How do you feel?

Next thing you know you are FINALLY checking out, with complete consideration for the people behind you and you walk out the door only to discover this woman, who had cut you off in line, has tripped on the curb and hit her face on the pavement. She is bleeding profusely, clearly in need of medical attention. You see people rushing to help her and there happens to be a paramedic who tells the woman that they will take her by ambulance to the nearest hospital. In desperation she explains that she cannot go to the hospital but that she absolutely has to get home to her daughter immediately. "Maria was just released from the cancer ward and has been given only a few days to live. Please, I cannot waste any more time. I'll be fine," she explains.

How do you feel now?

Attitude is everything. How you perceive and experience your life is completely and totally up to you and very much dictated by the habits you develop throughout your life. Reactions to what other people do and reactions to your own surroundings literally make your life what it is.

Consider how you usually tend to feel when people say or do things to you in a certain way. Do you more often than not choose to perceive people as "friendly" or "unfriendly"? Let's consider for a moment, how we act at home with our significant other or any loved one for that matter. Do you more often focus on your very own immediate worries, or do you frequently think about what your partner must be thinking? Do you know what they happen to be worrying about or thinking about at this very time? Do you tend to perceive them as overly considerate or somewhat selfish? Do you really know what's happening for them on the inside? Is it possible that you may in fact even influence what they think of you with your own perceptions? More than likely the tendency is to focus on your own worries sprinkled with frequent assumptions about what others might be thinking. And more often than not, you're probably not even close.

Let's take my husband and me for example. I frequently get frustrated when I come home and see what I consider to be a scowl on my husband's face while he is cooking or cleaning our house. He is a stay at home father which is his chosen job. I say to myself, "What is he so pissed off about? I just worked my butt off and he's been playing in the back yard with our daughter all day. How hard is that? Why can't he just smile when I come home? He should act like he's thrilled to see me and tell me how sexy I look as I walk in the door, looking spent. Why doesn't he run to the door and greet me as though he hasn't seen me in a month, like the dogs do? What is his problem?"

I start out being sweet with what I actually say to him, but after repeated attempts to get him to pay attention to my every word, I begin to get frustrated. I say things in an attempt to get his attention, such as, "Do you want some help?" Or I walk into the kitchen and begin making myself a snack.

This really makes him mad. And he snaps, "You could have just asked!"

At which time I snap back, "Well you were just standing there looking unhappy." And we are off on an annoying little rant.

Recently, I made the decision, as someone writing a book such as this must do, to talk to my husband about his less than cheerful greetings upon my arrival home from work. It turns out, he has not been mad at all. In fact, he is typically thinking about an upcoming race he is going to run which will require a tremendous amount of intensity. This naturally puts an intense look on his face. Suddenly the revelation hit me that when my husband asks me if I want this or that he is trying to put a smile on my face. Yet in a frequent state of deep thought about my own work, I fail to smile or even at times look up. What must he think when I forget to smile?

When it comes to our loved ones, we too often neglect the usual niceties that we would commonly offer others. People tend to let down their guards with the people they love the most, knowing that those people are somehow obligated to love them no matter what. Yet, wouldn't it be nice if we still treated the people we love with consistent respect and affection. Stepping this up just a little can truly make a difference. Moreover, when others treat us with less love and affection than we expect, a better habit than to get frustrated might just be to give them more love and acceptance. Their lack of attention likely has nothing to do with us. At the end of the day, the best thing to do is pick an opportune time to discuss it with your partner should you have concerns about what's on their mind. When in doubt, give more of what you want in return. If you want more affection, simply give more affection. If you want to hear more kind words, say more kind words. If you want more smiles, smile more.

GETTING BALANCE

"We don't have to think alike, to love alike."
~ Francis David

"Almost every wise saying has an opposite one, no less wise, to balance it."
~ George Santayana

Memories happen and I embrace them all. In the times when they are not what I had hoped, I remember to open my heart wider still, as without the sadness I presume there would be no joy.

Suddenly you wake up and have an abnormal realization that you don't really appreciate or enjoy everything in your life as you should or wish you could. You realize that every person in your life is their very own person. And you have to figure out what to do with yourself. Perhaps you are wishing you could spend more time with the person you love or maybe less. Maybe you realize you don't love your home life and you're trying to figure out what you could do today to make your life a better life. What now?

If you're like a lot of people, you may even question your own worth. You know you should have accomplished more by now. There are tons of things you know you could have done if you had just done this or that. You know on a deep level that you are special but you also know you are not tapping your complete potential, whether in life or in love. In fact, you go back and forth between a couple or sometimes many scenarios of what you should have been doing by now. Sometimes you know positively that you are undervalued by others. Other times you may even question how you've pulled it off to this point. You know that you are lucky and that others are much less fortunate than you. All of this and you are unsatisfied. You either work too hard at your relationship or you don't work hard enough at it. You are unbalanced.

Now what? You might start with a good laugh or a good

cry. You are OK. In fact, you are more than OK. You are alive and conscious of your surroundings and you are exactly where you are supposed to be at this moment. You have the ability to reflect and the capability to make changes. Look around and have gratitude for whatever it is that you do have. Especially have gratitude for your relationships. Perhaps even pick up a note pad and make a list of everything you are grateful for from the shoes on your feet to the food in your house to the options you have with love. You might take a moment to find beauty in the mess of it all and see goodness in the mass chaos of life. Give thanks for whatever it is that is right and perhaps for some of what is wrong. Begin by focusing on what good there is in your current relationships. Then go from there.

Let's talk specifically about your love relationships. If at this time you are feeling like you are doing more liking than being liked or more loving than being loved, step back to create a little balance. That means if you are liking someone too much or more than they are expressing towards you then step back in faith and allow them to come to you. Find within yourself the confidence to seriously back off and be OK with giving them their space. It is absolutely essential for balance. On the flip side, if someone is coming on a little strong, try letting them know. This will help them out in many ways. Nobody wants someone coming on too strong. Our tendency as humans is to run when someone comes on too strong, creating further chase and confusion by the other person. Why not help that person out by letting them know you need a little space. Spell it out for them sweetly.

If you are the one loving more than what is being reciprocated, focus on your self-confidence. That means you have to know that you are worthy, and be OK to walk away and be on your own. Know that you will be OK with or without this person who you love. Know that love is on your side and that everything worth having is worth admiring without a need for ownership of it. You are not in competition with others though we often fool ourselves into thinking that

162

we are. The truth is you are only in competition within your own mind. So drop the idea of competition and see yourself living the life you've always dreamed. Then give the universe space to manifest what you desire.

Life is a funny thing. It tends to deliver the positive side of that which we are least concerned about. Take a look at people who have a lot of money for example. People with money have little concern for money and therefore tend to be the people who get everything for free. They can afford to pay for things but oddly they don't have to. Slightly ironic, wouldn't you agree? Those people with plenty of love very rarely are concerned about love and tend to be gifted with the most dedicated of friends and lovers. To the contrary, those that worry, tend to manifest more of the things that they worry about in their lives. If you need to apply this to your love life, let go and let live. Begin your life today with the gift of confidence and watch as everything around you conspires to deliver to you the exact things you had only dreamed might be yours.

ON BEING SATISFIED

"Happiness is like a butterfly; the more you chase it, the more it will elude you, but if you turn your attention to other things, it will come and sit softly on your shoulder..."
~ Henry David Thoreau

Your life exists in a moment and each moment is a lifetime. Everyone is struggling to find satisfaction. Daily I ask myself, "What am I going to do with my life?" I'm frequently busy and hyper aware of whether or not what I'm doing is going towards the greater good. When it comes to having what you want, sometimes the best thing to do is simply stop striving, and start wanting exactly what you have.

Being satisfied in a relationship is not much different. Most of us have strong desires and tend to be perpetually dissatisfied.

It's actually a fairly small percentage of time generally that we spend in a state of bliss with anyone. Even when things should be fun when someone is in the pursuit phase of a relationship it often comes with jealousy, worry and moments of disappointment. Or you have won over the person you were pursuing and eventually that initial attraction wears off to some degree. When it's the latter you find other things to occupy your time, excite you and consume your mind. Rarely does someone stay perpetually happy in a relationship forever. If you're in the pursuit of someone who you think is the ONLY person who can make you happy for a lifetime, the truth is you will eventually bore of them too, to some degree. At that point, inevitably most of us say to ourselves, "What now?"

Most people would agree that to choose to live a spiritual life on some level, beats the crap out of not being spiritual. When you are spiritual, regardless of your faith, you can begin to see the beauty in even the smallest of things. It is a joy, for example to look at someone and suddenly notice something you've never noticed before, just because you've heightened your awareness for even a moment. Try it. Look at someone and notice something you've never noticed before. Seriously, you can look at yourself and do this as well. It may surprise you when you realize how much you weren't paying attention before. As a matter of habit people tend to fall back into a state of unconsciousness again and again. In and out, and again, in and out of consciousness and you know you are alive like all the rest of us. The more time you spend conscious or aware, the more you will enjoy your life on earth. There is literally beauty in everything around you right now. There is so much beauty in the mere imperfection of a relationship and in the mere imperfection of life.

Relationships are set up to be imperfect. They were designed by the master creator of relationships to be flawed, to be forever inadequate, and to be a work of art. They are forever changing. They never simply remain unchanged. It is impossible. The master relationship coordinators and creators probably have quite a sense of humor. They clearly love to be moved both to laugher and to tears. Relationships are as unique as they are plentiful, and for better or worse, with sweetness or in pain, they remain a work of art. An installation of live actors. This is true in all forms of life in fact. Watch any two or more species in a relationship and things are always changing. Always ugly or beautiful, completely depending on how you look at it.

My personal biggest challenge is in the acceptance of a daily routine in my relationship. While some love it, I simply abhor routine. I get bored easily and forget to notice the change within the seemingly monotonous repeat of each day. Yet, when I really stop and take notice, I see so much magnificence. My husband, my daughter and our dogs are never the same today as they were yesterday. Something is always new and beautiful but because it is often not extreme, I sometimes forget to take a moment to see it. Some days seem like a complete replay of the days before. Much like in the film <u>Groundhog Day</u>. Yet, when I stop, oh man, when I stop and really look, there's so much beauty to be found. Taking notice of daily change which is abundantly always happening all around us is what makes life satisfying.

INSIGHTS

Fixing Other People

1. All human beings have the need to be sincerely appreciated, accepted and loved.
2. When others criticize you it is not about you. Those are their issues, not yours.
3. When you criticize others, listen to what you are really saying. These are usually your issues.
4. Criticism does not create effective communication.
5. Sincere appreciation opens the channels for effective communication.
6. Most people rarely hear themselves criticizing others. Instead they believe they are trying to "help" others.
7. One of the greatest gifts you can give another human being is your unconditional acceptance of them.
8. With acceptance, you will begin to appreciate others more easily and small annoyances will disappear.
9. When you accept others as they are, you will be able to embrace the path that they are on without the need to control it and you will become an inspiration and a comfort to them when they need to grow. The alternative is a waste of everyone's time.
10. Unconditional acceptance, sincere appreciation and love will help to open the hearts of even those who appear to be unchangeable.

Other People's Attitudes

1. Nobody really knows what's going on with other people just as other people don't usually know what's going on with you.
2. Your perception and experience of life is dictated by your own habits.
3. Your reactions to what others say and do are completely up to you and will make your life what it is.

4. When it comes to our loved ones, we tend to take for granted that they will love us regardless of our attitude. Your loved ones however, deserve a good attitude more than anyone.
5. What others are frequently thinking about usually has nothing to do with us.
6. If you want more of something, start by first giving more of the very thing you expect. If you want more love, give more love. If you want more smiles, smile more.

Getting Balance

1. Everyone wakes up at some point in their life and analyzes where they should have been at by that particular point.
2. Accept that you are exactly where you need to be.
3. Have gratitude for what you have and where you're at.
4. Take inventory of your blessings and make a note of what is beautiful in the mess of everything.
5. If you are loving more than you are being loved, back off and let love come to you.
6. If you are being loved more than you love or you are feeling smothered, tell the person who is coming on too strong how you feel.
7. You are not in competition.
8. Life delivers the positive equivalent of that which you are least concerned about.
9. Let go and let live. Trust and life will deliver to you your wildest dreams.
10. Know that love is on your side and that everything worth having is worth admiring without a need for ownership of it.

On Being Satisfied

1. Everyone is struggling to find satisfaction. This is not

unique to anyone. All humans are perpetually dissatisfied.
2. Make it a practice to find beauty in small things.
3. Notice something new about someone you look at every day.
4. Notice something new about yourself.
5. There is so much beauty in the mere imperfection of a relationship, the mere imperfection of life.
6. Relationships are always changing. Getting better or worse. It is impossible to have a relationship without change.
7. Everything is always ugly or beautiful, completely depending on how you look at it.
8. There is always something new and changed in everyone every day. It is a matter of habit for someone to stop and take notice.
9. Taking notice is what makes life satisfying.

11

Spelling It Out, A Life Fulfilled

SETTING UP OTHERS
FOR SUCCESS WITH YOU

"How does anyone ever spend a lifetime together?
Easily: One moment at a time."
~ Julieanne-ism

One of the most beneficial things I ever did for my husband when we first began dating was to create a key. I titled it "The Guide to Understanding Julieanne." It went something like this. If I <u>SAY</u> "THIS" it really means "THAT." Also, if I <u>DO</u> "THIS" it really means "THAT." The list was long. It included specifics of not only word choices I might use but also actions that I might take, with definitions for what my meanings truly were. Without the list the only way my husband could have possibly succeeded in communicating with me would have been, if he had been a phenomenal mind reader. I'm so happy I spelled it out for him.

Here's the thing about women, we don't always say what we mean. In all fairness to our partners, creating a key can really set our partner's up for success when dealing with us. If everyone created a key at the start of their relationship, there would be a lot more successful longer lasting relationships in the world. The idea being that you gift your partner with an easy way to understand your methods of communication. This is not telling them everything about you in the sense that you would take away your own mystery. It's about creating a better understanding of how you operate. It was funny because I decided to write this section and said to my husband, "Hey honey, do you remember that 'key to me' that I gave you many years ago?"

He replied with "Heck yah! Are you kidding? I still refer to it." He quickly pulled it out and handed it to me. He had actually kept it all these years. He let me know it was a valuable tool in understanding how to please me.

Let's face it, all human beings are unique and have their own idiosyncrasies. Guessing is one way to learn to communicate. However, imagine if you were handed a key to your partner's secret methods of communication. Would you not feel as though you had been granted a foot up or been given a head start?

Spelling It Out for Your Man started out many years ago as I observed myself repeating the comment, "spell it out for them." I frequently said this while counseling close friends on how to improve their relationships. It was obvious that most people had the power to change their own circumstances, by taking responsibility for their own judgments and styles of communication. The common problems I witnessed were textbook repetitive from one relationship to the next. I noticed early on in life that one of the most frequent causes of relationship problems between men and women, stemmed from women expecting things of their men, that the men had no way of knowing. I used to wonder how in the world a woman could expect something from a guy that he had no insight to. This was especially true considering the men rarely read between the lines like the ladies did.

Truthfully ladies believe they can read between the lines, yet they really don't do it that well. Women tend to read into things in such a way that their imagination takes off soaring. By the end of an interpretation of something simple a man said or did, a woman may have come up with something that didn't even slightly resemble what the guy actually intended by it. If you did a key for a guy it would be short. It would say... Key to a GUY: "What I say... Is what I mean." *Unless of course the guy is a liar.*

If you are in a newly committed relationship and you are serious about making it last, consider providing a key to your partner. Or ask for one from them. It really can make all the difference.

LETTING YOUR PARTNER
BECOME WHO THEY TRULY ARE

"Don't believe what the eyes are telling you. All they show is limitation. Look with your understanding, find out what you already know, and you'll see the way to fly."
~ Richard Bach

Fear can be a powerful force. It can scare or it can teach. It can push or it can lead. It can shrink you or it can build you up. When faced with "love" fear, there is only one choice. Jump into the middle and surrender. Embrace your journey and spread your wings and you will see that only good comes from love, never anything to the contrary. People speak of hurt and bitterness from a broken heart, yet true love will not leave a broken heart. True love never dies. It never ends. True love is grounded completely in trust and makes no demands. "Love" and a "relationship" should not be confused as the same thing. Love exists without stipulations, without prerequisites, without bitterness and without expectations. While a relationship is the act of two or more people learning to communicate and be with one another. A relationship is always in need of constant and conscious adjustments, yet love only grows and exists. Love never lessens. Have faith in love and all else will happen by the force of nature.

Love should never be limited, contained or withheld. Even when you get married, there will be attractions that you and your spouse have to other people. Freedom to love without limitation is a dream. Each of us is an exceptional creature and there is nobody else like any one of us on earth. That is truly magnificent. You are a human being and what guides you and makes you the most extraordinary limitless human you can be, is a little thing called love. The more you give of it, the more it will come your way. Loving should be allowed to happen freely while relationships need to be defined and expectations within a relationship should be spelled out and mutually agreed upon. Love need not even be spoken of, to exist.

If no human being is like any other then what we each perceive as right or wrong is as different as we are, even if we trained from the same school of thought, were raised by the same parents and went to the same school or church. You will never find two people on earth who agree to the exact degree on every subject matter. It does not matter if the subject is abortion or how to drive a car. There are varying degrees on every level to which we each feel more or less strongly about aspects of each detail of every subject. In addition, we often change our thinking throughout time. Human beings have a tendency to try to influence, even force people to behave the way they think that they should behave. Parents do it with their kids, kids with their parents, wives with husbands, husbands with wives, siblings with each other and friends with friends. People do this for many reasons. The reasons vary. Sometimes it's because someone annoys someone with their habits which they feel should mimic their own, or sometimes because they are simply embarrassed by them.

Most of us have this pointless urge to want our loved ones

to look good or act a certain way when we are trying to impress people. We want our significant others to say the right things around our bosses or parents or whoever it is that we are not completely ourselves with. This may make sense with children while they are learning certain societal boundaries. Imagine though, a life where the only reflection of you was the one of how you yourself acted or behaved. What if no other human being regardless of their relationship to you, had any influence on how people looked at you? Each person was only a reflection of themselves. What freedom we'd experience. Imagine that you stopped trying to change your significant other's behaviors, you allowed them to truly be themselves, and you embraced them for it. Moreover, imagine someone allowing you to be completely yourself with no contrived demands of your conduct. Don't get me wrong, in relationships people need to spell out their boundaries so as to understand what is expected of them. However, once baseline expectations are set and agreed upon, self-expression should be encouraged, and love should be free to give and receive without restriction. And certainly no one should ever be punished for feeling love.

If love is limitless, then there is no need to contain it and jealousy should cease to exist. Jealousy is the result of crossed relationship boundaries and is not a result of love. Love has no end. Love needs no boundaries.

TRUST

"Faith is knowledge within the heart, beyond the reach of proof."
~ Khalil Gibran

Trust is not hoping your partner will love you. It is KNOWING that they DO, and letting go of the need to make anything of it. We all want to believe we are special and we are. And we aren't. What makes life enjoyable is to live a little bit more by faith every day. It is scary when it comes to loving someone to think you could possibly be replaced by another person, but there are a lot of people in the world, and you cannot predict the future. What you can do, is love, then love some more.

Just as the rain carries positive ions, so does change make you more apt to experience love with an expansive heart. There is good in everything and everyone. Attachment is vital to caring and nurturing but non-attachment grounded in faith allows all goodness to return to you.

When it comes to love, your point of view, your imagination and your energy can carry you through anything. As you love, it will spill over to everyone and everything you encounter and beyond. There is no force imaginable that is more powerful than the act of love. If you want to speak to someone you cannot touch, see, or hear, the voice of love will transmit with or without a phone. It crosses all borders and travels through time and walls. Some say ignorance is bliss, I say love is.

If your intention is to gain anything, become anyone, or to soar beyond your wildest dreams, the way is love. If your desire is to have peace, or to have freedom, the way is love. If you want to grow, strengthen, or heal, the way is love. And if you love, all things you've ever imagined will become possible.

INSIGHTS

Setting up Others for Success with You

1. People don't always say what they mean.
2. If you want to have a successful relationship, help set your partner up for success by giving them the meanings to what you say and do.
3. It is unfair to expect others to guess what is expected of them.
4. Everyone has different ways of communicating.
5. Women especially tend to say one thing and mean another while men simultaneously are not generally good at reading between the lines.
6. Women have a tendency to read into things when often there is truly no added meaning to the things that men say.
7. Spelling out your meanings for your loved ones will help you to achieve greater success in your efforts to effectively communicate.

Letting Your Partner Become Who They Truly Are

1. If you have fear when it comes to love, jump into the middle and surrender. Only good can come from love.
2. True love never dies. It never ends. True love is grounded completely in trust and makes no demands.
3. Love and a relationship are two different things. A relationship requires boundaries but once set and agreed upon should be left at that.
4. Relationships do require consistent adjustments as people are always changing.
5. The more you give love away, the more you will receive it.
6. Love only grows.
7. No two human beings are the same. All people have different perspectives. We all have different ways of

seeing every subject.

8. People have a tendency to try and force their loved ones to behave the way they themselves would act in social situations for fear of embarrassment. Nobody's behavior is a reflection of anyone but themselves and all people generally speaking should be allowed to be themselves.
9. No one should be punished for feeling love.
10. Love is limitless and need not be contained.
11. Jealousy is not a result of love. It is a result of crossed relationship boundaries. Love and relationships should not be confused.

Trust

1. Trust is not hoping your partner will love you; it is KNOWING that they DO.
2. Live by faith and life will become enjoyable.
3. You cannot predict the future but you can love and then love some more.
4. There is good in everyone and everything if you choose to see it.
5. Non-attachment grounded in faith allows good to return to you.
6. Love is the greatest power there is.
7. Love travels and should not be contained. It is limitless.
8. With love, all things are possible.

AT LAST

...In a state of panic at having discovered that his princess had run away, the young man ran out of his empty home calling after her. Knowing that he was willing to do whatever it took to make his wife happy, he began scouring every inch of the town in hopes of fixing whatever wrongdoings he had committed.

Meanwhile, the beautiful princess could be found tucked away, hidden in a quiet corner of a quaint local book store, reading a powerful book titled, *Spelling It Out for Your Man.* At last the princess went running out of the store, only to smack right into her Prince Charming knocking him out cold in the street.

As he slowly came to, he could hear his wife murmuring something softly.

"My love, my love." She went on... "Art has one purpose, that is to leave you changed. Love has one purpose, that is to create art. We are artists my love. Let's go paint a spectacular life together."

And they lived happily ever after.

THE END

ABOUT THE AUTHOR

A spokesperson in business for many years, author, actor, friend, wife and mother, Julieanne O'Connor insists on saying what's on her mind, and asking the questions that people never thought they'd be asked, regarding love and sex. The shocking consistency of answers in both private and public are the inspiration for <u>Spelling It Out for Your Man</u>. After researching couples for over fifteen years, including business professionals, co-workers, friends and strangers using questions designed to evoke candid replies on the secret to a happy relationship, Julieanne has extracted the keys to what appear to be the cause of today's many unhappy marriages, and failed attempts at love. A not-so-quiet observer of men and women with their consistently repeated mistakes, Julieanne O'Connor is determined to break through the highly prevalent taboo of sharing some of what's really going on in the minds and hearts of men and women, regarding sex and love.

SpellingItOut.com
Facebook.com/SpellingItOut
Twitter.com/SpellingIt
Pinterest.com/SpellingItOut

CPSIA information can be obtained at www.ICGtesting.com
Printed in the USA
LVOW06s1159050214

372461LV00001B/103/P